WORDS

Joy

Love

Laughter

Pain   Tears

WORDS

WRITTEN BY
MICHAEL DAVIS
12/2021

ISBN: 979-8-88589-879-9

Printed in the United States by Morris Publishing®
3212 East Highway 30
Kearney, NE 68847
1-800-650-7888

DEDICATION

I WANT TO DEDICATE THIS BOOK TO MY
SON (MICHAEL KEVIN SIMMS). FROM
HIM AND GOD, I WAS ABLE TO COME UP
WITH THESE WORDS TO TOUCH EVERYONE.
ALSO, I WANT TO THANK MY BEST FRIEND
FOR HER INSIGHT AND INPUT WITH SOME
OF MY THOUGHTS. THROUGHOUT MY LIFE, I
HAVE SEEN AND EXPERIENCED A LOT AND
DID NOT ALLOW IT TO STOP MY GROWTH.

LOVE AND PEACE

ENJOY THESE WORDS OF ENCOURAGEMENT AND INSPIRATION, MUCH   OF THESE WORDS ARE INSPIRED THROUGH A LIFE OF JOY AND PAIN. THEY ARE PUT TOGETHER FOR YOUR NEED OF ENCOURAGEMENT. EACH MONTH IS FILLED WITH UPLIFTING QUOTES AND PRAYER.

W= WORDS

O= OFFERS

R= RELIEF

D= DURING

S=STRUGGLES

CHAPTER 1-12

269 pages with 37,662 words of greatness….

Chapter 1   January

January the beginning of the year.

JOY = LET NO ONE REMOVE THE JOY FROM YOUR LIFE.

ATTITUDE = MAKE YOUR ATTITUDE REFLECT

YOUR DREAMS AND GOALS...

NEVER = NEVER GIVE UP ON YOURSELF...

UNSTOPPABLE = KNOW THAT ONCE YOU ADD

GOD IN YOUR LIFE YOU BECOME UNSTOPPABLE.

ABILITY = YOU HAVE THE ABILITY TO DO

WHAT YOU SET YOUR MIND TO JUST

BELIEVE.

RICH = YOU ARE RICH WITHIN YOUR SPIRIT AND

BELIEF IN GOD.

YOU = ITS NOT ALWAYS ABOUT YOU.

I made it, yes, I made it. I am one of the chosen ones and if you are reading this you are too. Welcome to Fantastic Friday. We going to start this 2021 off differently. this is F_____ Friday. (everyone, make that (F) what you want it to be. fellowship Friday, forgiving Friday. Dear God, I want to thank you for laying your (Footsteps) for me to follow that I can make it out of that (Forsaken) land and b with my (Family). I want to forever thank you for forgiving me of my wrongful ways. I will (Follow) you to your kingdom of peace and love. Thank you for (Freeing) my mind that I can understand. Dear God it is in your name we pray... AMEN, AMEN, AMEN.

Spectacular Saturday. Today is a different day, today we take our next step to healing, cleansing our inner spirit, strengthening our foundation with our righteousness that we can stand strong. facing our fears and looking beyond the unknown. Dear God, I ask you to be my eyes and your angels be my protection and your everlasting love be my guide. it is in your name we pray. AMEN, AMEN, AMEM.

Once again, we have been forever blessed to make it to super Sunday...super Sunday has so many healing powers I don't always know where to start. Dear God as we pray for strength u reach out and touch us, as we pray for warmth in these cold times you blanket us within your arms, as we pray for peace, you smile upon us shining your bright light of love and redemption. thank father for being so kind to us, AMEN, AMEN.

My, my, my it's a magnificent Monday. My blessings grow and grow as I (MOVE) closer to God. You don't hear me. My blessings grow and grow as I (MOVE) closer to God. what does that mean, well it means we need (MORE) of God in our life. I don't have to get there when it's free b4 8 pm. I don't have to have on polo nor Gucci, see God has no dress code nor price, come as you are and he will let you in. Thank you, dear God, for keeping your doors open 24/7 365 days a year. thank you, God, thank you. AMEN, AMEN, AMEN

Tuesday, Tuesday... Trusting Tuesday. we have put our trust in so many things and it has let us down, when have u put your trust in God... When... Well, it's time you put your trust in your creator the one that has gotten u this far...

Workshop Wednesday, in your workshop we are building a better you (me). So, let's gather the tools we are going to need. First, we have to find the true (you), then we are going to need to look through you and find our (God), now once you and God get together, he will say where is your (understanding), so you and God find understanding hanging out with his friend (belief), so, to your surprise belief said we need (faith) because without him God can't do the work in the workshop to build a better you. Here comes faith laughing saying, at last, you have brought us all together in this wonderful temple uniting us once again now let's go tell it on the highest mountain (thank God almighty we are free at last). When you take your body to the workshop of God, he will fix it. AMEN, AMEN, AMEN.

Let God's children say AMEN for he woke us up on this TREMENDOUS THURSDAY. I want to take you back again into (throwback Thursday). See we live in a day and time that is full of chaos. God woke you up but when are you going to (WAKE UP). We have forgotten the ways of our fathers, teachings, it's like we living in an earthquake, the ground is falling apart beneath us. Lets' put these families of love back together. AMEN, AMEN, AMEN.

Gm Friday… We are men/women upright, independent, and fearless. Who care for their loved ones and follow the prophet to a destiny which is not uncertain nor unknown They are fortified by the impregnable doctrine built upon love, truth, peace, freedom, and justice.
As we move in the science of unity and love let God guide us and keep us loving each other today because tomorrow may not come for some. AMEN, AMEN, AMEN.

Gm Saturday. My son said it is better a patient person than a worrier. Patience gives u all the advantages of using all your strengths not just your muscles. One that thinks can figure out and get around the obstacles. So today we pray for patience and willpower to remain in control and not out of control... AMEN, AMEN, AMEN

Gm super Sunday. My mom says it is spiritual Sunday well let's look at it. Your spirituality is yours. Your connection with your God. but first things first. We first must come into the knowledge of self. (self-worth, self-love self- knowing self-control, and then unselfishness). See the one time it's about self you lose focus, you can't comprehend, you can't hear. In order for your spirituality to reach its highest level, you must learn about yourself. For when you level up on self you are connecting with that breath within your God. He is that mighty force inside you that wakes you up. That keeps you going, that makes you love unconditionally. See your spirituality will help you make meaning of your life, will give a purpose in your journey, will define the ways of your character. When you find yourself. You will find God standing there. AMEN, AMEN, AMEN church say AMEN, AMEN, AMEN.

Gm Monday. There is a fight going on in your building. Between (right and wrong, good and bad, sinful and righteousness) this fight takes all the energy out of you because sometimes you want to fight on both sides. It is ok because when someone gets you wrong you have to get them right, and some days you just can't get away from being bad so somebody has to show you the good in you. So, in all of this, we have a (CHOICE). So, people, my first choice is God. I'm choosing God for then I'll be victorious. I pray too that he continues to help us. AMEN, AMEN, AMEN

Glory, glory, glory on this blessed THANKFUL TUESDAY. Gm the doorway or should I say the pathway to God is open.
Come one come all for there is a place for you with God. The only fees are (trust, faith, devotion) the people put on a dollar bill (in God we trust) they put on your medicine (take one by mouth twice a day) they put on cigarettes (may cause cancer) we trust that dollar, we follow that prescription, and we that smoke devote our life to cancer. don't laugh because God asks for nothing less than what
these (items) say but he gets less of us when we want more of him. Let us hold hands and walk this path to God and watch the blessings start to unfold. I

thank you wonderful and merciful God for love and life. AMEN, AMEN, AMEN. Say it like you mean it AMEN, AMEN, AMEN.

Welcome, welcome, Wednesday. Don't you wake up and go reaching for that nicotine and caffeine before you thank God for getting you here at this moment. We always got to have something other than God to pick us up, to get us going. none of which outlast God. That will be gone and u will want more but God he will always be there never running out of stock, never a shortage, never a season of drought... My God comes with a never-ending, supply hers better than the Energizer Bunny. Take a dose of God a breath of fresh air, a boost of energy, she is pound for pound the greatest there has ever been. My beloved brothers and sisters welcome God into your life get your affairs in order today with God. He is your wake me up in the morning, and take me to rest at night. AMEN, AMEN, AMEN. Have a wonderful day on God loves you all.

THANKFUL THURSDAY... We are children of the highest We are direct descendants of a higher power we have inherited DNA from greatness. our birthright says we are headed for greatness so hold your heads up high today tomorrow and days after because not only is God watching he is with us. I want to thank God for life and all of his blessings. AMEN, AMEN, AMEN.

Friday, Friday, Friday. Finding Friday, what did you find out yesterday that happened today? Yes, God is still blessing you. Within God's paradise, everything becomes new. Today I want you all to tell God what you're thankful for on this great Friday. Dear God, I am ever so thankful that I'm not the same

MICHAEL I once was. I'm thankful that you came back for me and rescued me from the hell I was living in. I'm thankful for every breath of fresh air you allow me to breathe. AMEN, AMEN, AMEN. What are you thankful for? Have, a blessed day love you!

It's always a blessing to open my eyes to another day. Satisfying Saturday. We here now let us get up and do something with this blessing. Don't let this one pass you bye. Life is not as long as we think so live it, love it, enjoy it, open your eyes and let God show you the wonders of the world he created through his guidance. Have a blessed day.

Super Sunday gets your body jumping. jumping for God because without him we wouldn't have made it. My mom says its sample Sunday, I want to know when will we be done with the samples. I'm tired of trying this trying that I want the main course I want a full helping of God. I need a long-time fix, not just a taste. I want the full directions to God, not the side street, see I'm done with trying it's time we get it done. Dear God, please hear me I come to you in need of a better way and with you I know it's a better way

Gm meaningful Monday. Making meaning of your life and all you do. This means having and taking responsibility and control of (u). So, with this attitude, one is sure to grow and prosper in life. Dear God I come to you for guidance and help, I seek you first and only for I know through you I'm sure the outcome. I owe you all the prays and glory. thank you, God, for your blessings.

Gm testimony Tuesday... I have one for you today. God has been so good to me. When you have been in a dark place and the light comes u know God is good, when you have felt so beat down and you are still standing on your feet you know God has been good to you. When all you could do is cry and now you are smiling God has been good to you. God is good all the time ... Thank you God for always being there for me. AMEN, AMEN, AMEN.

Gm workshop Wednesday. bk to the basics. The workshop of the heart, mind, soul, and spirit. We are constantly working on the outer appearance that we forget that there is more to us than what's to see. Your heart needs cleansing, your mind needs to be open, your soul must know it's worth saving, and understand your spirit is one with God. Dear God as we enter your workshop gives us the strength to stand the course endure the time it will take. I thank you, God, for your undying understanding. AMEN, AMEN, AMEN. have a great day.

Gm terrific people. Welcome to Trusting Thursday. I am turning things around for a moment. I have a question. (CAN GOD TRUST U?) Yes, I asked. Now you want to know why I asked. Well, when things not going well, we ask (God why me) when we can't have it right now, we ask (God what's taking so long) God needs to know no matter the time or way you still believe, you still have faith, not questions. He is not like Santa clause wanting to know if you have been good or bad to be there for you. He is a constant in your life now you be a constant in his. TRUST in your God, he is always working for you now let's go to work for him. AMEN, AMEN, AMEN.

Gm Friday. freeway Friday. We are on this freeway and our FREQUENCY is off. You don't hear me. We have lost our connection with God. We are so concerned with our WiFi connection but not our connection with God. We need to reset our FREQUENCY to the right channel to find God's station, we need to tune in to what he is saying to us. with all that's going on, there is a message, lesson in it all. My brothers and sisters let's get back on the right FREQUENCY with God.

Gm searching Saturday, Forever searching for that pot of gold. Understanding that your thirst for more never ends the higher you go you want more, the more you can accomplish the more you want, our unique design makes us want to grow mentally physically, and spiritually. never lose focus, never forget who you truly are, and always put God first and you will forever climb. AMEN, AMEN, AMEN

Super Sunday. I am just a man doing the best I can to maintain a balance of physical, mental, emotional, and spiritual health. As we take our journey on this road called life we struggle, but within our struggle, we gain strength from our great God. Through him, we are able to maintain our strengths. I pray we maintain our connection with God to help us balance our true selves. AMEN, AMEN, AMEN.

Always know you are stronger than your fears and wiser than your setbacks. Always look forward. bless you

Gm meaningful Monday. My prayers are going up for us all. Your thoughts are key to your success. Clean up your thoughts, empty out your wasteful energy, remove your hateful images of destruction, illuminate the damaging obstacles in your mind, then you can replace them with meaningful tools for success. A must-do make God the beginning and end of all you do. Feed your thoughts the proper foods God and more God. AMEN, AMEN, AMEN. Have a blessed and meaningful Monday...

Gm to you. Thank you so much God for waking us up and getting us started with tempting Tuesday. Yes, these days come I'm tempted by the devil's delights. Pushing us to fall

off course. Through my praying warriors, I'm able to maintain the course. moving forward and remaining strong. I know some days it's hard and you want to just give in, this is when you pray harder, and hold on. The devil sees peace and is always there to interrupt it. DONT let him maintain control of your peace. Love you all to peace and blessings... AMEN, AMEN, AMEN.

Gm to (Working it out) Wednesday... WHY work it out. Well, as God bless you every day with life. You begin it with different challenges. Some of us fail the very first challenge because we forget to thank God for getting us here, then you fail the second one because you start with and about what someone else did, as the third one come you immediately fail it because you start blaming others for your (BS) (sorry), so I'll stop you here and ask that we all say (THANK YOU FATHER FOR BLESSING ME WITH LIFE), then look in the mirror and say (I LOVE U) NOW GET YOURSELF TOGETHER AND GO HAVE AN AWESOME DAY BECAUSE GOD LOVE US ALL ... it is ON (U) AND ONLY U TO SEE IT. I SEE MINE. LET US GET TO

WORKING WITH GOD NOT AGAINST HIM. BLESS YOU.

Gm my tenacious people. Welcome to Thankful Thursday. Being thankful can take you a long way in life. Today is all about being thankful let God know you are ever so thankful for your blessings and his mercy. AMEN, AMEN, AMEN.

Gm freeway Friday. Today is for filling Friday. There is a lot to be fulfilled and as we drive on this glorious freeway. We

must pay close attention to the road signs they are constantly changing your direction putting you on different roads but it's YOU that must maintain the course. Each day is the beginning of a new life. a seed has grown. Live your life grow your seeds and always make God first. AMEN, AMEN, AMEN

Gm satisfying Saturday. Let's take a look at our week. meaningful Monday, tempting Tuesday, working shop Wednesday, thankful Thursday, freeway Friday. All these days leads us to today when you have taken all the steps, the complete dosage, drove down all the right roads you will be forever satisfied. With God in control, we are destined for greatness. AMEN, AMEN, AMEN.

Good, good, good morning super Sunday. Those of you that's up glad you made and those that didn't may you rest in eternal peace. Let's get up and do something for your God. praise him, show him your love for him, glorify his name, let's have praise where you stand. Heavenly father creator of all things I want to thank you for all that there is you have done for us. I ask you to rain down your cleansing water upon us, I ask that you clear the air that we can breathe, take off these blinders so we can see you clearly, open our hearts and minds to receive you. It is in your name we pray. AMEN, AMEN, AMEN. Have a great day and stay safe love you all...

Chapter 2

February

February is the shortest month of the year yet it is the platform for black history...

FREEDOM = FREEDOM IS NOT FREE, IT COMES WITH A PRICE OF EMOTIONAL, PHYSICAL, AND SPIRITUAL PAIN.

ENTHRALLED = DON'T BECOME SO ENTHRALLED WITH THE ILLUSION OF FREEDOM.

BONDAGE = YOUR MENTAL BONDAGE IS JUST AS BAD AS THE PHYSICAL BONDAGE.

RUN = RUN FROM EVERYTHING THAT WILL ENSLAVE YOUR MIND, BODY, AND SOUL.

UNDO = UNDOING THE PSYCHOLOGICAL IMPACT OF SLAVERY WILL TAKE A LIFETIME OF MANY.

APPEARANCE = WE ONLY APPEAR TO BELONG IN A SOCIETY THAT IS UNJUST TO OUR KIND.

REACH = ALWAYS REACH BEYOND THE BOUNDARIES YOU ARE CONFINED TO.

YOU = YOU WILL ALWAYS REMAIN THE GIFT

Gm Meaningful Monday, well as we make meaning of things, we dedicate time and energy to different things every day for some the same thing every day. but we only use time and energy for God once a week on (Friday, Saturday, or Sunday) for some. But now God makes time for us every day all day. I have a question for u all (who do you love?) Think about it. now as you go down your list (I love my mother, father, kids, siblings, wife, husband, BFFs, etc.) no one said God first. The real MVP of life comes in at a close 5th place for some. I want you to understand that God always put you first and now it's your turn to put him first. Let's say it together. Dear God, I come to you first and say I love you father, I come to you before all others because I know you will help me work it out. Once again, God, I love you. AMEN, AMEN, AMEN. My people as your day begins and ends remember to tell God you love him. I love you all be safe and peaceful. AMEN.

Gm Trusting TUESDAY. Today I want you to know that there is a power within you that can take you beyond your wildest dreams. You just have to connect with that motivating power. we just know how to call on God when we are in need of something. We can't and don't understand what it means when the (BOOKS) read (you are created in the image and likeness of God) (God breathed the breath of air into you that you may live) you need to connect with that God within you. That divine strength that has been dragging (U) around all your days. We are quick to want to be addressed as Kings and Queens yet we act like lost creatures. God gave you dominion over everything yet you can barely rule yourself. learn to trust that strong voice inside its God talking to

you. Love you be safe and blessed.
AMEN, AMEN, AMEN.

Gm Work it out Wednesday. We are
constantly in a workout with the (mind,
body, and spirit) we should forever be
feeding the temple of ours a complete
healthy diet. (Knowledge, exercise, and
spiritual love). I challenge you all to a
healthier life. Dear God guides us to a
healthier life to a for filling future. full of
your love and mercy. AMEN, AMEN,
AMEN.

Gm thirst full Thursday. there's a well
that's full of healthy nutrition. We have a
natural appetite for love, knowledge, and
direction. our thirst drives us it pushes
us to limits that we find unreachable only
because we want to fly not walk. When
we take life in its stages. We get the
fullness of what we thirst for. Portions
make us understand things clearly. Let's

take a pause and slow down take your time don't be in such a rush, and that what you wish for will come to you. Dear God I come to you for patience and understanding. That I may see the joys that pass me by so often. and that you forever be our protector. AMEN, AMEN, AMEN.

Gm Freeway Friday. Today is all about Freeing yourself of all the Chains, Shackles, and blockages that hinder you from moving forward in life. We don't know that we place these items on others with our mighty but also nasty TONGUE. Dear God as I learn to remove these painful items out of my path, I ask you to help me get them out of my heart. As you help me break these chains of fear and disparity replace them with the courage to face all life's ups and downs. Amen. We often use the titles of being KINGS And QUEENS know what it means and begin to live as such. Be blessed and have a Wonderful Friday. love you

Gm to this Satisfying Saturday... I am a repeat offender, I failed to learn the lessons of history and now I'm repeating them. Haven't we been told, shown, and heard that disobedience to God ends with destruction. We must start listening and following the laws and ways of God. " You are the children of one father, provided for by his care, and the breast of one mother hath given ye suck. Let the bonds of affection, therefore, unit thee with thy brother that peace and happiness may dwell in thy fathers house ..."AMEN, AMEN, AMEN. Remember your relationship with each other love before you hate. Have a great day...

Gm KINGS AND QUEENS. WELCOME TO SUPER SUNDAY.

Today is all about energy. Within the universe there is good and bad energy, within people there is good and bad energy, and inside you also. So, today we pray that we are protected against this bad energy and we ask God to help us receive the good energy. See that good energy brings about a power within you, it gets you to moving around doing positive things. It makes you want to live and love life. It makes a rainy day bright. Put that good energy in your cup of coffee this morning and have an outstanding day. Much love.

Gm meaningful Monday. Making meaning of your life is always a constant thing. As we bring super Sunday with us into Monday, we allow the positive energy to continue on.
Today tell someone something positive and good not just you love them but something to lift them higher

than what they are. So, I'm telling you all you are worth it, you are worthy of God's love and blessings. Be true to yourself and love yourself, you are Gods, gift to humanity. Lots of love, AMEN, AMEN, AMEN

Gm Thankful Tuesday. Those that are reading this have a lot to be thankful for. As I strive to keep my positive energy flowing. I ask for your help Gods and Goddess. Dear God I ask that you put in my mind the thoughts and understanding of success, put in my heart the desire and hunger for achievement, put in my hands the tools and strength for productivity and peace, and place upon my tongue the words of love and righteousness. With these blessings, you may release into your world to share your love and mercy. AMEN, AMEN, AMEN. You all be powerful and united in spirit. MUCH

Love and respect

Gm WORK IT OUT WEDNESDAY...My beloved brother and sisters come walk with me, walk with me into a life of healthier living. (SPIRITUAL, PHYSICAL, MENTAL AND EMOTIONAL) Yes, we are on our positive journey for a greater and longer life. I want you to take 5 deep breaths then breathe yesterday, bad energy out into the universe. Now say thank you God for helping me to work it out. come walk with me. As always, I pray for the strength to continue on. I want you all today to be encouraged and know that God is leading our walk, be blessed and if no one has told you they love you. Know that God and I love you .... AMEN, AMEN, AMEN.

Gm Trusting Thursday. today I trust and know I'm not alone in this sometimes cruel fight of life. for today I know my

God is with me. my God pulled me out of a first pit and molded me into the man I am today. I want you (reading this) to know and trust that that same God is doing it for you right now. TRUST and know he will never forsake nor forget you. Dear God I trust and believe in the works you are doing for us and we thank you for these blessings. AMEN, AMEN, AMEN.

Gm Freeway Friday. Who is ready to take this ride with me? Today is about loving yourself. Put the time and energy into you Stand up and say God I want to live now your ride begins. Get your (Qur'an, Bible, Karan etc.) And pray. Now throw out the window your (negative energy, bad thoughts, weaknesses, misunderstanding, all the thing that kills the body-mind, and soul), and replace it with the gift of life. Learn how to feed yourself the godly nutrients you need.

Find your peace and let no one take it away. Dear God I want to thank you for the strength and courage to take this wonderful ride with you, I'm in need of healing that can only come through you, I ask that you send your angels down to protect us on this ride. AMEN, AMEN, AMEN much love and welcome to a ride to a healthier life...

Gm Satisfying Saturday... I want to dedicate today to the WOMAN... Dear God I want to thank you for creating humanity (the woman). For through her comes out future and love. I want to thank you for letting us see your beauty in the flesh. AMEN. Now to you QUEENS I say thank you for those that don't know-how for it is you that help balance the sadness of today, it is you that has become the strength of our families today. I want you to know that you are one of God's greatest gifts to man. Know your true worth and understand that it does not come with a price tag, know that you are more than just a pretty face. You are the captivating hands and minds of our past present and future. I can never thank you enough for standing so strong when I have failed. Today I say to you, you're KINGS are bouncing back and we will give you a man worthy of your greatness. So, I just want to thank you always for being that soft but ever so strong voice we need. blessings to you beautiful women. Much love and respect.

Gm SUPER SUNDAY. Today yes is a super day to give all the thanks and praise to God he empowered u to make it through. Today I want to give a special tribute to the (MEN) I want to thank you for being a Father, a Brother, an Uncle, a Grandfather, and a Friend. I want to thank you for always trying even when you were not sure what you were doing. I want you to know that you are needed, we need you to get back up and be that King God designed you to be. I know you may not be told as much as you should but I recognize your efforts. give that man a hug today and let him know he just got to keep trying. You are appreciated. Dear God I want to thank you for the MEN you have molded-in your likeness for giving him that anointing power to endure all the heart ships he must face. I want to thank you, God, and God, I ask you to continue blessing him with your love. AMEN, AMEN, AMEN. As a man I want it known that we r trying and I'm going to stand strong and b that (Man-God) in the face of the ones I love. To the MEN God is watching you.

GM, GM, GM. How are you on this Meaningful Monday? We are always making meaning of our lives, who we are, and where are we headed. My life is dedicated to doing the works of a righteous good man, who am I, I am a child of God sent here to give you a message, where am I going, I'm headed for greater things in life by abiding by the laws and principles of God. So, we pray to God to give us insight, hindsight, foresight on this journey. Today do things that give you meaning, speak things that give you understanding, and see things as they should be. Have a blessed and loved day. knowing somebody loves you. (GOD AND ME) AMEN, AMEN, AMEN.

Gm Trusting TUESDAY. Dear God, I have witnessed your mighty work, I can bear witness to your love and mercy, I thank you God for showing me the truth. AMEN, AMEN, AMEN. We have put trust in many different things and have been let down. We need to rewind and reread the history lessons. become a part of today's future. (our kids) Give them someone and something to trust in with no errors. let's step up (Father's, Mother's, brother's, sister's etc) We need to become their role models and guidance not the tv nor the play station. Dear God gives me the power and strength to accept the things I cannot change and the courage and strength to change the things I can. (ME). AMEN, AMEN, AMEN. Be great in what you do today and do it with love. Love you.

Gm holla if you hear me. Welcome to WORKING IT OUT WEDNESDAY. As the saying goes (won't he do it, won't he do it). As God works things out for us, we must work things out in us. (Who you with the coach yelled) I'm with you God, yes, I'm with you God. If you are on God's team let me, get an AMEN. Being on God's team you got to (act right, do right, stand up, speak up) see God sent prophets to us, messengers to us to give us the way. Now it's our turn to be the message. so, let's work it out and get it right. AMEN, AMEN, AMEN. As always, I leave with peace and love. be great champions.

Gm Thankful Thursday. I am so ever thankful to God each and every day he allows me to breathe his fresh air. God, I just want to say thank you. Thank you for every lesson and blessings you have given to me. People, it's not always about where you are going but more about how are you going to get there. The roads you are going to travel. Pay attention to the road signs just as you will the road. Go the speed limit not too fast you may miss something important, not too slow because your blessing can pass you by. God is forever with you be sure to be with him. Love you, stay safe and warm it's cold in these streets. Lol AMEN, AMEN, AMEN.

Gm, it's FREEWAY FRIDAY. Thank God for this day just as we do the other days, he has blessed us to see. Freeway Friday is all about you freeing yourself of the unseen (stress, pain, hurt, loss, disappointment, etc.). It's time to work on you. Self-motivation, growth, love is some of the things we strive for. get in touch with your inner spirit to bring forth your brightest shine. You are a gifted and amazing King/Queen. Dear continue to ride with us on this journey of life with all your blessings. AMEN, AMEN, AMEN From the darkest night to the brightest day we will shine. Love you all.

Gm Satisfying Saturday. In order to be satisfied, you must first want something.

As in a painting, I painted he want to be (RELEASED). The message today is about Freeing yourself from that which holds you down. We never know what someone is facing until we ask. Check on your loved ones even if it's just to say (gm, gn, how are you etc.) Dear God, we come to you today asking that you release us from all sicknesses mental, physical, and emotional. We ask to strengthen the weak and provide for the less fortunate. AMEN, AMEN, AMEN. I know everyone has their journey to travel just know you are not alone. God is forever with you. You have the power to be great now go be awesome. much love and respect...

Gm Super Sunday. Dear God, we come to you and give thanks to your mighty works, for giving us the knowledge and understanding that it takes for us to change to become a better image of you.

AMEN. I want to say to (U) readers I am proud of you in your journey towards change, in your efforts to change into a better version of your true self. I want to say it is amazing to see the growth and development of that God inside you. Keep doing what you doing and know that there is always a light in that dark tunnel. Just as the butterfly transforms into its true self, he also went through stages but he came through flying beautifully. Know that you will too. My readers give a hug today of love and have a blessed and caring day. AMEN, AMEN, AMEN.

Gm Meaningful Monday. I pray that all is well and under the care of God. For being under the care of God there is no sickness he can't cure. As we continue our journey on self-evolving know that there will be some dark moments, the devil will forever be trying to keep you from growing into your God-self. I believe in you, I know u got the strength to continue on, hold your head up high and b proud of your growths and your failures for they define u within the way you handle them both. Know that u have and will continue to come out on top. Because you got a mighty God riding and fighting with you. Dear God, we can never thank you enough for the blessings we receive but we will try every day to show you by doing your work. AMEN, AMEN, AMEN. (TIME NEVER WAS WHEN MAN WAS NOT. KNOW THY SELF AND WHEN U THINK YOU HAVE STUDIED ENOUGH GO BACK AND STUDY SOME MORE, FOR YOU ARE FOREVER GROWING.) LOVE YOUPEACE.

Gm Trusting TUESDAY. Dear God thank you for your mercy. We are creatures of habit we do things over and over again and some of the things we do wrong. Not because we don't care we just were never shown the right way to do it so it just continued on. So, today we are correcting a lot of wrong learned behaviors. Young boys pull your pants up that's wrong behavior, young girls put some less, revealing clothes it's wrong behavior. Your look is your first impression then it's your, speaking. Let's work on building a beautiful you. love you AMEN, AMEN, AMEN.

Gm WORKING IT OUT WEDNESDAY.
Dear God I come to you thanking you for the courage and strength to fight my demons. From the beginning of the fall of man, he has been in a constant fight with his inner demon. Free will has given man freedom to choose right or wrong which stirs up an inner conflict. Man/Woman must face their inner animal to see who will rule your temple.

Continue your fight pray and pray some more. Self-improvement is something we strive for every day. So, grow spread your wings, and fly asking God to help you beat the beast within you. Put on your godly armor today and fight for good. Be your own superhero today. AMEN, AMEN, AMEN love you.

Gm Terrific Thursday. What makes today so terrific... (YOU) and the reasons God allowed you to see it. Every day is a test of your fortitude within living your life. Today look around and take a moment and see your blessings. Peace be still. love you... be patient, be aware, be caring, and forever be in prayer. Peace and love. God is good all the time. AMEN, AMEN, AMEN.

Gm Satisfying Saturday. There is a great satisfaction that comes over you when you are doing right and it also comes with a lot more obstacles to get around. Satisfying your inner soul and spirit can raise your level of spirituality. You must apply dedication, study, understanding, and faith. Dear God help me to overcome my weaknesses and wrongful intent. Continue to give me the strength to travel on my path. AMEN, AMEN, AMEN. Have a safe and wonderful day. be good to others the universe is watching. It does return.

Gm gods/goddess, a blessing to you on this great Super Sunday... Dear God, we thank you for your guidance as we travel and grow. we thank you for providing the path to you. AMEN. (readers) there comes a time when you are going to say

(I surrender to you God) being in the light is so warm and peaceful. Because we know being in the dark is cold and scary. Grab hold of your soul and your spirit bring them together and let your mind be free. God has a plan for you, you, you, and me, let him in your WHOLE life not part but for your WHOLE life. Be ever grateful and loving in all you do. peace and love

Chapter 3

March

March is the ending of the cold winter and approaching spring, the beginning of new life.

MESSENGER = GOD ALWAYS SEND HIS WORDS

THROUGH MAN.

APOSTLE = SENT FROM GOD.

REBEL = WE RISE AGAINST THE WAYS OF

THE WICKED MAN.

CHAOS = CHAOS IS IN THE MINDS OF THE

WICKED.

HELP = HELP IS ON THE WAY

Gm Meaningful Monday. Have you made meaning of URSELF? If your answer is yes then you need to stop what you are doing and look in the mirror. We make meaning of things, events, and situations, that have occurred in our lives. When it comes to self we are forever growing and changing with every event and situation within our lives. As you witness gods, blessings you change and grow closer to your understanding of your God. As you cross milestones in your life, you grow within your belief and faith. All these things give meaning to your life and understanding of your (self) ability. Dear God as you continue to send your fighting angel here to fight for our weary souls and to uplift our weakening spirits, we thank you for keeping us elevated and wrapped in your love. We can never thank you enough but we can show you our gratitude by sharing your love for others... AMEN,

AMEN, AMEN. as always be kind to others for they may be your key to your salvation... Love U...

Gm Trusting Tuesday. I trust that you all are growing while on your road to building a better YOU. God has given us all that we need to do the work it's on us to perform the task. Dear God every day I come to you thanking you for your gift of life, for the small things we take for granted such as the flowers and the rain. For these ever-so-little things help us in life. the rain washing away the air pollution, and the flower reminding us of your beauty. We thank you father the moments of silence to help us focus and see our blessings.
AMEN, AMEN, AMEN Travel in peace and share your love.
Gm Working it out Wednesday. How are you working things out, Dear God thank you for this day is the beginning of a

better life and way of life. Change is going to come.

Gm terrific Thursday. WHAT MAKES THIS DAY SO TERRIFIC? For me I'm still here God has blessed me with the strength to see another day. AMEN, AMEN, AMEN
On this terrific day, I want you to take focus on the SUN. Does the sunshine no matter what condition the weather is in. It may be behind the clouds but it is shining. The sun will rise and it will fall (go down) We are like the sun we rise and at times we fall but the sun raises back up some of us don't we get so broken we give up. If God continues to wake you people never give up keep rising and shining like the sun. You're a beacon light to all mankind so shine, shine, shine. love you

Gm Freeway Friday. back on the road again. God has blessed, many road highways, and crosswalks that we have taken. All, of which has led us to this very moment. You feel like you have been hit by cars, bricks, other people, and stepped on broken glass, but you are still here standing stronger than ever. There is a reason for this. you are chosen every day when he wakes you for a purpose. Now get up and be a blessing as he has blessed you. Dear God, I thank you for every moment you give me to do your work. AMEN, AMEN, AMEN. Much respect and love

Gm satisfying Saturday... I'm up and I feel like dancing. In like comes a tremendous amount of pain. Physical, emotional, and spiritual. because we often feel let down, left out, but this only comes from you being selfish, you want it to be all about YOU. Well, it's not. See when you need help you get down and ask God " please make a way for me " and he does. he sends your help by way of somebody else. then you get back on your high horse until you fall again needing help. So, today we will give help instead of wanting help. Dear God thank you for the chance to be the blessing you created me to be, thank you for loving us through our pains and for fixing them. AMEN, AMEN, AMEN hey you get up and move something. love you!

Gm Super Sunday. the day we set aside to worship God. I feel that each and every day is a day to worship God and thank him for his blessings. We put things in categories. which is fine but where do you and your God fit in these categories. We go from, I have to do this and I have to do that. Well, make time every day for you and your God. He and

You are more important than all that you must do. give your God a shout-out. give yourself a hug. thank that man/ woman in the mirror for being that godly image. then thank your God for always helping. Dear God, I'm shouting from the highest mountain top thank you. thank you. AMEN, AMEN, AMEN. Won't He do it? I applaud u all in your efforts to be God-like in your actions and words. bless you and always much love!

Good afternoon. Meaningful Monday. Thank you, God, for helping me make meaning of this life. We give meaning to all things related to our life. Now understand these things don't give meaning to you, you give it meaning. That outfit doesn't make you, that car doesn't make you, you make these things stop putting objects above you. We are the reason for it all. through God, this is how it became what it is. stay focused on yourself and God, not the objects. Much love peace. AMEN, AMEN, AMEN.

Gm Trusting Tuesday. Today I want to bring your attention to value. Your value, God created you in his image this in itself gives you higher value than what money could buy. Our value system is off so let's bring it up to the level where you can understand it yourself. Your value is not determined by your amount of money but through your core value system. Your character, your actions, your God-like ways give you divine worth. Have a blessed day and let raise our value system get it in order

Gm Working it out Wednesday. Dear God I come to you today asking for your shield and protection as I work things out in my life and this world. AMEN, what are you doing today to work things out in your life? I'm growing my mind, spirit, and understanding of my god. Inside of my worldly life building my brand (ME). always work on you. AMEN, AMEN, AMEN. Be blessed and focused. love U!

Gm Terrific Thursday. Dear God thank you for this day holds many treasures that are here with us and one that's home with you watching over us. On this day as we take a look at our value and worth, let us now learn to never take for granted those that are worthy of our value (time, space, air, love) for these things will one day be no more to us. Today we live in joy and peace. Letting nothing stand in the way.
Be happy and blessed today. Love you AMEN, AMEN, AMEN.

Gm Freeway Friday. I am free. free of all the Chains, and Shackles, (mental, physical, emotional, and spiritual). My mind and heart are clear of all bad energy and now I'm able and ready to receive all that God has for me. These are your daily words. Dear God thank you for clearing and freeing up my soul and spirit that my journey will be easy. AMEN, AMEN, AMEN. Be good to others because roads meet up at other points to help build bridges. love you all be great always.

Gm Satisfying Saturday. Here we are on this beautiful day. Thank you, God, for this blessed day. Today is a day of peace. peace of mind-body-soul and spirit. be at peace today. Be blessed and enjoy your day. love you.

Gm Super Sunday. my god is a super saving and loving God. Dear God, I thank you for your undying love and mercy. I only ask what can I do for you God to show my love for you. AMEN, AMEN,

AMEN. Stop what you are doing, look at how uniquely you are made. Being cut from a worthy and divine cloth. You were designed for greatness. The universe has favors for you. So, it is time for you to get up and get to working towards your greatness. Be super in all you do. Blessings are yours always. love you.

Gm Meaningful Monday. Dear God, I thank you for giving me the understanding that I can focus on my purpose in life with that came my meaningfulness to life. AMEN. when we are making meaning of things in our life, we must look at first the reason then what was the lesson these can give meaning to all situations. Stop being so into what happened but see why it happened. what was your role in the lesson we are so quick to say what was the other entities fault that we don't see our own activity making meaning of your life means taking your responsibility to all that you do be blessed and responsible today for the world needs you at your best here's a hug now go be great Love you AMEN, AMEN, AMEN

Gm Trusting Tuesday. Today is trusting that you are not alone in this life. I know days come and go and u have this emptiness inside but you are not alone. Trust and believe that however, you feel God is there with you. He is holding you up and that person you think just doesn't understand well he/she does they go through it too. Dear God thank you for knowing how and when to send your angels down to help and sit with us we thank you for filling that ever so empty place in us with your love and comfort. AMEN, AMEN, AMEN. be at peace with the world today for everyone needs to know somebody cares. Here's a

huuugggggg now pass it on someone
is in need of one. Love you.

Gm Working it out Wednesday. Dear God
on this wonderfully made day I thank you
for your blessing of life. AMEN. What are
we working out today people? Let's work
our way out of some restraints. Work our
way out of the things that hold us back.
We are the people who CAN not the ones
who can't. If your reading knows you are
the chosen one. Chosen for greatness.
Just have faith and believe in yourself.

Gm Terrific Thursday. Dear God, I want to
thank you for pouring your rain down upon
us to clean the air to wash away some of the
germs. We are in great need of cleaning.
cleaning out our minds, hearts, bodies, and
spirits to be replaced with your likeness.
AMEN, AMEN, AMEN. we always need a
reminder when it comes to doing what's
right. Why does wrong come so easily? As
before we have been shown wrong so often

that it came habit. This must change. Reach for right and don't fall to the wrong. By the way you yes you, you are amazing much love and respect. Peace!

Gm Freeway Friday. Dear God thank you for giving me a path to follow as I try to be a reflection of you in man. I thank you for my journey. AMEN, AMEN, AMEN. Today all I want to say is GROW UP, MAN/WOMAN UP, AND STAND UP FOR GOD AND WHAT'S RIGHT. PEACE LOVE U!

Gm, here we are Satisfying Saturday, what makes Saturday so satisfying, you see it. You are here with us still enjoying the blessings of breathing. Dear God, we thank you for your most precious gift (LIFE). A blessing sits in front of you, (untouched, not received). A gift walks by u (out of reach, not understood). God spoke to you (you didn't hear, you were not listening). We pray that God help us, yet we are blind, dead, and dumb to the messages, signs, and works he sends our way. Riddle me this, (if a picture is worth a thousand words why we don't get it when we see it) open your heart, soul, and spirit God is knocking let him in. Have a great day be blessed. Love you Peace.

Gm Super Sunday, we are here in this moment of greatness, we are bearing witness to God's wonderfulness, (LIFE). Yes, he has given you life. A life to live to the fullest. Now for some (to the fullest) is interpreted in many different ways. God means to your highest potential, within your gifted talent, your greatest ability. See in your God-like self. Things are immaculate. Dear God bless me on this day just as you have on days before and the many days to come, mold me unbreakable in the worldly storms that I shall face, keep me comforted in the pain this life will bring, and forever keep releasing your angels of righteousness to watch over us. It is you we submit to God. AMEN, AMEN, AMEN. Be forever blessed and give uplifting words today as you enjoy Super Sunday. love you

Gm, Meaningful Monday, what is the true meaning of (love, devotion, belief, faith)? These words have been greatly missed represented by man/woman. We use them as they are kites flying in the wind with no direction. As I have said before we have been taught wrong so long, we have made it the new right. Dear God, we ask for your guidance especially today to correct our ways, get us back in line with the truth, bring us inside the structure of righteousness, and help us to love. When you love completely when you believe without fear, Faith has the strongest faith ever, and when you are devoted to something, be devoted in honesty. Be proud of who you are, be great at working to who you can become, always strive to be better than yesterday. God has shown you the way. Peace stay safe... AMEN, AMEN, AMEN.

Gm Trusting Tuesday. Ok, let's get into (trust). trust is established over periods of time yet it is easily broken in seconds. We need to be careful of how and whom we trust. In God is where we need to get our guidance from and with him our trust should be. Dear God, I put my trust in you.
AMEN, AMEN, AMEN. Peace .

Gm Working it out Wednesday. it's a great day God has blessed us once again to have a chance at serving him (God). no matter the difficulty God is there and his angels are there helping us work it out. Be diligent in your work and study of God and self. be blessed love you

Gm Terrific Thursday, How, are you all doing this blessed day? God has a purpose for you. You are great and don't even know it. You don't see that you are winning because you pay too much attention to others' life and not yours. Look at where you have been, what you have been through, and inside your own storyline if you don't see a winner something is wrong with you. God gave you better days and you spent them shopping and watching your blessings go by, God gave you rain to wash away the germs and you complain of pain you couldn't see the trees and flowers growing. God has always given you and the moment he takes something you ask why. We want to talk to God now. Well people we need God every day so start talking to him he is listening. Thank you,

God, for always hearing our prayers and for providing for us that which we need. AMEN, AMEN, AMEN. Peace and much love always.

Gm Freeway Friday, this freeway ride is made just for you.
You will get off of unconscious lane and take understanding Blvd, at the intersection of can't see straight crossing and give me a fix junction you will pick up Mr. wisdom. He will have directions to better days court, or won't he do it valley. There you will begin your study at the self-redemption hall. As you leave behind you all these roads of destruction, keep your head in the books of growth. Here you will see the manifestation of the god in you. Sometimes on your road, you must have a tour guide that will help you find your way as well as you giving them help. Pay attention to your guide, read all your

signs. God got you!! Much love and safe travels. Love you!

Gm Satisfying Saturday, Dear God thank you for providing for me the things I need and not my wants, I also thank you for giving me the understanding to know the difference. Amen. We often get these two confused with each other we put our wants above our needs. Being satisfied is simple, having a focus and purpose will satisfy you dearly. Stay focused on what's important, give purpose and value to things of great importance. Stop wasting time and energy on waist full things. OPEN YOUR EYES, TUNE YOUR EARS, AND CALM YOUR TONGUE. BE GREAT AND AT PEACE LOVE YOU.

Gm Super Sunday, there is a unique design in how we are created. Have you really ever taken a look at how we are created? We grow, we brake and we mend back together, we think, we feel, and we are nurturing. Over time we have separated from who we are. We have walked away from our source of energy that worked for us. Now we are dependent on drugs and medicines. Some, how some way we must get back that energy we once had. That fire to live. God wants us to live. Dear God I want to live. I want to live in your likeness and guidance. Strengthen my body for it is weak, comfort my soul for it resides with you, and brighten my spirit that the world shall know God lives here. AMEN, AMEN, AMEN. let everybody say AMEN. Give a hug show your appreciation for life. love you. Peace.

Gm Meaningful Monday, making meaning of things is so important. Making meaning of things allows us to prioritize those things in their proper place. As we grow to a greater understanding things become less important than others. Most importantly as we grow, we realize that our spirituality becomes of the utmost importance. What are you making meaning of today? In your process of making meaning of things be open-minded and diligent. I pray you to a great understanding of life. Peace love you AMEN, AMEN, AMEN.

Gm, Trusting Tuesday. Today we are in a great trust that God will provide all we need. We just need to pay attention to the things and people around us. Our perception of things isn't clear because we don't see with our god's eye. Clear your perception and use your god's eye it works. Trust God and have a blessed day. Love you. Peace .

Gm, Working it out Wednesday. How are you working things out in your life today? My path to this day is I now put God first. God starts my day and ends it. With this method, I'm able to remain focused on the duties of my day. Nothing should be above your God. As we thank him for his blessings, we open ourselves to more blessings. Living in life in a righteous way we expand our spiritual wealth and spiritual health. I'm am noticing that in this day and time we need some of our old way of life back. The family unit as a village, the family love, and structure, where we did things together. (Eat, shop, read, pray, and most of all LOVE). I pray you all are back to spiritual health, wealth, and love. AMEN, AMEN, AMEN. Peace .

Chapter 4

April

April, let God shower you with his rain of love that you live a great life.

AGAINST = AGAINST ALL OBSTACLES YOU WILL

     STILL RISE VICTORIOUS.

PROGRESS = PROGRESS IS ONLY ACHIEVED BY

     MOVING FORWARD.

REWARDS = COMPLETION IS YOUR REWARD
FOR YOUR DEDICATION AND HARD WORK.

INSPIRATION = LET YOUR INNER GOD BE YOUR
DRIVING FORCE.

LOVE = THROUGH LOVE WE ACHIEVE AND LIVE
LIFE

Gm Terrific Thursday, as the rain washes away the poisons in the air, we should step out in it to wash away some of our dirt. Today is about making your life terrific and it starts with yourself. We need to get rid of all these toxic ways, toxic thinking, toxic people. Refresh your life with all things good and wholesome. Let's learn how to eat to live and not live to eat. Eat the words of God, the food of God. Dear God guide me to a better life, allow me the knowledge to grow up. AMEN, AMEN, AMEN.

Gm Freeway Friday, It's a cold day today. Once again on our journey to a better life. A better life doesn't mean you will be rich in dollars and cents. See rich people aren't happy they just make you think they are because you not rich in dollars. See I have a spiritual, physical, and emotional richness and will allow no one to take it. I can run out of money but the source of richness I'm tapped into the supply stays on overstock. If you are diligent in what you want it's coming. So, I wish you well in your journey to richness. God first always. Peace AMEN, AMEN, AMEN. love you

Gm Satisfying Saturday, learn how to satisfy yourself. I have a question, (why do we (humans) look for destruction. Is it the inability in use to not believe that everything is all right Or is it that some of us feel better inside of chaos Well, it's not healthy Now God said let there be peace on earth Dear God please give us our peace back help us save the mindset of our youth they need healing. God. I know you have sent messenger after messenger to lead us out of chaos it surely is time for one now. AMEN, AMEN, AMEN. Peace LOVE U

Gm Super Sunday, we look for a hero to come and save the day for us. Someone that will step in and make things better, but some of us don't know when help has arrived. We don't get the help we want we get the help we need. Know what the difference is. Open your eyes and see when help has arrived. We are creatures of habit and we miss a lot when we can't see. open your god's eye to begin seeing clearly.

God loves you and so do I. AMEN, AMEN, AMEN Peace .

Gm Meaningful Monday, giving today meaning means giving thanks to our great God for his wonderful blessings that he passes out every day. Be forever grateful for God's love.

Have a blessed and fabulous day. Peace and I love you.

Gm Trusting Tuesday, every day is like the beginning of your life. A baby's cry is a scream of joy (I'm here at last). Forever learning growing exploring until our fears begin to slow them down just as we were done. Why slow down the growth process we crave as a child. Reach out and grow and grow some more. There is so much to learn in this world. Free your mind and take it in. Learning new things refreshes your life. Dear God free my heart and mind of this fear of living and let me live my best life following your guidance. AMEN, AMEN, AMEN. Peace love you!

Gm Working it out Wednesday. In all realms of life, there are things we will be working out. This life prepares us for the next journey. I use to wonder why grandparents would say he/she has an old soul or they had been here before. So, in this universal life it's truthfully said there is nothing new under the sun and karma is real. Be strong in what you are working out and true to the matter at hand. You are one of many chosen to do the work for God. Stay safe and blessed much love Peace.

Gm Terrific Thursday, your day is made terrific by your doing. God starts you off and you step in and do the rest. (What's in your heart?) Stop waking up with what happened yesterday. Start your day with a positive prayer, be the director of your emotions, be the controller of your actions. As God to allow you to use his strength to continue on. If no one has told you, know this, I believe in you, I know you can do whatever you put your mind to doing, and I'm proud of you. You are beautiful love you and have an awesome day on God. AMEN and Peace.

Gm Freeway Friday. Let's break this down (free-way) the word free means it cost you nothing, the word way means a means or direction. Now on this freeway journey though there is no monetary value there are risks. The risk factor comes when you think you can do it alone, you don't pay attention, you don't ask questions you are just riding along blindfolded. There is so much that can distract you that staying focused is very important today. Dear God cover me with your protection, lead me with your voice of guidance and comfort me in your arms of love. AMEN, AMEN, AMEN. Now you yes get up and move something lol have a great day ... PEACE love you!

Gm Satisfying Saturday, Dear God I want to thank you for this blessed day. May the warmth of your sun rays blanket the earth with your love. AMEN. Trusting in God will keep you forever satisfied. As we continue on our path of self-improvement, he will guide you and his angels will protect you. Today take a moment and love on yourself because you are amazing. love you Peace.

Gm Super Sunday. What is so super about today. (1) God has awakened you from your sleep, (2) God has forgiven you for yesterday's sin, I can go on and on. Let's look at his awakening you from your sleep, when God wakes you are coming out of a dream that was awesome, you were on top of the world so he stepped in and woke you for you to get started on that journey. Not for you to look around and say that was just a dream he woke you to make that dream a reality. Those mistakes you made before he has forgiven you for them now, you need to forgive yourself. We stay stuck because we can't let go. Let it go let nothing slow you down nor hold you back. You are gifted and HIGHLY favored so let's make these dreams come true. Dear God I ask that you inject me with the desire to succeed, to fuel me with the energy to get the job done. Nothing is possible without you and ask that you be with me every step of the way. It is in your name we pray. AMEN, AMEN, AMEN. Be humble and peaceful, much love and respect. Peace.

Gm Meaningful Monday, today is the day we make meaning of things within ourselves and life. We gather events and actions among other things that help us come to desiring factors about yourself and life. Never once do we attach our own actions to the meaning That mirror image of you gives you the meaning and reason you are how you are. Know that everything starts with you and God. Be great at working on you then we can build a world of God-like people. Dear God give us the ability to face ourselves. AMEN, AMEN, AMEN. Here's to life let's live it.

Gm Trusting Tuesday,

T= TAKING

R= RESPONSIBILITY

U= UNDERSTANDING

S= SELF

T= TREATMENT

this is my trust. With God, I can do the necessary things to better my conscious, subconscious, and unconscious state of being. We must expand our spirituality so that the other areas of us will grow. Our connection with the almighty creator will empower you with a force that will take you places no man/woman can take you. Let's get bake to our godly birthright quality. Dear God as you continue to bless the readers of your message open their eyes, minds, and hearts to become empowered with your love and devotion. Send out your protecting angels to keep them safe and blanket them with your shield of armor that they remain forever guarded. AMEN, AMEN, AMEN. much love Peace.

Gm Working it out Wednesday. As we stand on the battlefield of life some fights are overwhelming, some are rough, and some breaking points in our life. There is nowhere written where it says it will be easy but it does tell us we are not alone. On your battlefield, you will build character, dignity, self -respect and add value to your life. On this battlefield, men are made women are formed and some will forever remain broken. Pay attention to your life be kind and productive and surely God will bless you all of your days. Dear God, we thank you for this day, the sacrifices we have made, the lessons learned, and the days and journey to come. It is you I want beside me on this battlefield of life in your name we pray. AMEN, AMEN,

AMEN. if you find yourself in need of help, just call him. Much love Peace.

Gm Terrific Thursday, today is an amazing time to be living. We are in a time that has pushed us into a close-net environment with the ones we love (family). In this time our patience is tried our commitment is tested our faith is called upon. Hold on for this battle of life shall pass also. I just say love and love hard on those you love. Pray more to strengthen your faith. Dear God as you strengthen me in these times. I want to thank you, thank you for keeping my loved ones safe. AMEN, AMEN, AMEN. Peace love you...

Gm Freeway Friday. Roads, rivers, valleys, highways, streets, ponds, lakes, and the open skies are means by which our physical body will travel in life. Now conscious, subconscious, unconscious, intuition and imagination are means by which our soul and spirit will travel now we aim to connect the three together soul body, and spirit that they can take these journeys together. Once we learn how to unite them, we become the hero we are in our dreams in reality. Your true source of energy and strength lives within you. Stop locking it up when you wake up from your sleep. You want your dreams to come true but once God wakes you in the morning you put your dreams to sleep. Let your dreams rise with you. Work on them in your day-to-day life not just your sleep. Warm that engine up (your mind) and get to work at being your greatest you. God loves you and so do I. PEACE.

Gm Satisfying Saturday, Dear God we come to you in thanks to seeing this blessed day. There is no power greater than yours and it is your power I seek.

Amen. How can you be satisfied when your wants, needs, and desires are all over the place, We, are so distracted by things we lose interest in the other. This is where you find your strength in your God to help you maintain your life. This is where we need a balanced diet. Food for the mind, heart, soul, and spirit. Just as we have our basic four food groups, we have parts of the human design that needs feeding as well. Give yourself the balance it needs. For your mind give it the knowledge it needs to understand, your heart, give it the love it needs to survive the pain it will feel, your soul surrounds it with joy and peace, your spirit connects it to your creator and never detach it. I thank you all for giving me an audience to talk to. Tell someone thank you today. Be good and peaceful love you. Peace.

Gm Super Sunday. I want to talk about praising your creator, for we believe that we have to go to a physical dwelling (temple, church, mosque) to praise. We think we have to be in a large group. Well God allowed this pandemic to prove you don't. He gave us time to work on our family, get involved with what our children are doing, to rebuild what was in place years ago. God is everywhere so we are able to praise him anywhere. I want you to know that God looks good on you. Yes, he does. Let your God inside you shine. Open that window and let your God flow. Tell that person next to you that God looks good on them. Look in the mirror and tell yourself God look good on me. Dear God I want to thank you for being the most important part of my every day.

Thank you for following me around. AMEN, AMEN, AMEN. love you and once again God looks good on you... Peace.

Gm Meaningful Monday! Dear God I see your works, I feel your presence, I understand and receive your wisdom. Amen. Today I want you to open the window to your entire being to the powers and works of God. As pray for a greater life we shall act out in a better manner. Our world has been poisoned with a wicked mindset. We have sat around watching life change. Do we not hear the cry for help in our people ways, What is the meaning of this We come from a time of loving each other today of war right in our own community We need a change and a change is coming, but we first must change back to God Be at Peace and learn to love not to hate Peace much love.

Gm Trusting Tuesday, Dear God, I trust you with my life for without you there would be no life. Amen. Trust is gained over time and broken in seconds. Once you have gained the trust of someone you should honor it as you trust in your God. Our loyalties are screwed up. We have loyalty to materials more than we do people, we have lost our way in the sight of God yet we pray every day and ask for forgiveness. Get on track and stay there stop falling off. God never falls off on us so let's move toward him and stay the course. Be great today and have a blessed one. Love you Peace.

Gm Working it out Wednesday. Yes, we got some things to work out today. We are ever grateful for the verdict of guilty yesterday with the Floyd case. Yet it is not a victory when we kill each other at a higher rate. From the way I see it for every 1 cop that kills a black, there are 20 other blacks killing another black. We hate and kill each other more than any other group hating and killing us today. When do we get back to protecting our own Your life matters to me who life matters to you Dear God help us to see that we are valuable, we are needed, we are strong.

Gm Terrific Thursday, (MASKS) we have been wearing masks for many years. Our personalities, characteristics, our ways are just some versions of the masks you wear every day. Hiding our true selves from the world. (The wolf in sheep clothing), (the friendly snake that wants help out the road). Deceptions we come in contact with on a daily basis. This is why we ask God to help us work on ourselves that we can be our true selves. Help us see the wolf and snake for who they truly are. I want you to stand up and be proud of who you are and that beautiful skin you are in. God created you uniquely. Dear God help me do away with these masks and false images of myself, for now, I know I am a child of the highest and He accepts me as I am. As you begin to learn your true self watch the power that comes through. I pray for your health, wealth, and strength. AMEN, AMEN, AMEN. God loves you and so do I. Peace

Gm Freeway Friday, let's get our free way of being together.
It's free to love yourself. It's free to love and follow God. It's free to be respectful to yourself and others. These natural things in life are free so why do we put a price tag on them. Everything we have that should be given and done freely we put a price tag on them are we that greedy for a dollar that we have to change the free liberties of true nature. God freely loves you and gives his mercy to you freely. Dear God forgives me for my greed and allow me to freely give myself to your works. Amen, AMEN, AMEN. love you Peace

Gm Satisfying Saturday. Dear God let this day be the day that riches fall from the sky.

Let your sun rays brighten everyone's future. Amen, AMEN, AMEN. Now that God has done his part it's on you to do yours. Now get up and do something great even if it's telling someone that you love them. Understand that actions bring about change and progress. So, put your biggie woggie shoes on, and let's rock. I made you smile, didn't I. Have a great day God loves you and so do I. Peace

Gm Super Sunday, Made from clay and molded into a man. Man fell from his place on high when given a choice. Man chose poorly so now he is forever trying to regain his place with God. So there came many messengers with the lessons of God that man should follow to get back in his righteous place with God. So today as some fellowship remember why we do so. God continues to send messages to us to help us along the way. Be joyous in your praising him and staying focused on God.

Dear God, I thank you for the life you render to me every day that I can do my best because through me you appear to mankind. AMEN, AMEN, AMEN. Show kindness
to all for God loves us all. love you and Peace
Gm Meaningful Monday. Dear God as I speak to my people allows me to be powerful and received. Allow their inner ear to hear me and their soulful eye to envision what I'm saying. AMEN, AMEN, AMEN. You are strong though seen as weak, you are a survivor though left for dead, you are beautiful though you have ugly ways, you are smart though you speak foolishly. Why and how do we know these things but still choose to be on the worse side? Today you take control of yourself. Your duty to God is to live your life on the greater side of it not the bad. I say to you, you are beautiful, you are amazing, you are a child

of God let no one tell you anything different. love you Peace

Gm Trusting Tuesday. God trusted us to be fruitful and multiply not destructive and killing. God gave us dominion over a sacred land yet we treat it like a wasted land. He gave us the right foods to eat yet we eat poorly. God has given us his bright sun rays that strengthen us yet we try to block it out. God has given and continues to give what are you given in return. Dear God I give my obedience to you, I give thanks to you, I put my trust in you just as you have done me. AMEN, AMEN, AMEN. You have an outstanding day and love on those that love you. PEACE

Gm Working it out Wednesday. Let's work this here out. not only in the last year but days and weeks also in times of the past we have gathered in remembrance of a loved one or friend. Well, it's not fair to that loved one nor the friend that we can only remember them when we can know and love them now. Share your love today, not in remembrance. Today make a phone call or text and tell the ones you love that you appreciate and love them. Dear God as you work on me allow me to work for you. Dear God, I love you and appreciate the life you have given me to live. AMEN, AMEN, AMEN. Hey, you yes you I love and appreciate you too.

Peace

Good afternoon on this terrific Thursday. Dear God, I thank you for your continuous mercy and love. I thank you for waking me and giving me the strength to move forward in life. AMEN, AMEN, AMEN. The saying "I want for my brother that which I want for myself" sounds good, even as it comes flying out your mouth so smooth that you believe it. In some parts it's true but what if that same brother only shows you nothing but bad. This is where the true test comes in. God says live him still but you can do it from afar. You don't want anything for yourself so it is hard to give him the fruits you want when he just wants a handout. We must surround ourselves with like-minded people. People that love God and people that believe in themselves. Men and women surround themselves with warriors of God and the best is yet to come.

love you and Peace

Gm Freeway Friday. Dear God, I want you to know that I am truly grateful for your continuous love. I am truly thankful for each day you allow me to take a deep breath of your air. AMEN, AMEN, AMEN. As we continue on our journey of growing a better you, I want to remind you of the things that come for free. These freedoms we lack in having in these days and time (gm, excuses me, how are you, thank you, have a good day, etc.) These things are free but we lack the respect to render them to others because we feel entitled, that the other person should do it first. Have you even told God to thank you this morning for his blessings of life? Let us remove these barriers that divide us. We may not think alike but we share a common interest. We may not pray alike but we are praying to the same all-powerful creator. We may not face the same troubles but the pain is real. Acknowledging people before things are very important. I acknowledge you. You do matter to me and I love you. This too is free. PEACE Have a free-filled day and be great.

Chapter 5

May

May is when all the beautiful things that God creates come full bloom.

MAGNIFICENT = GOD'S CREATIONS ARE WONDERFUL AND MAGNIFICENT.

AMAZING = GOD'S WORK IS AMAZING TO SEE.

YOU = YOU ARE CREATED IN HIS IMAGE AND LIKENESS

Gm Satisfying Saturday. Today is all about winning. Dear God, I thank you for all these blessings that are coming my way. I thank you for the victory. Through you, I'm always winning. AMEN, AMEN, AMEN. Today I see you as a winning, a true success, you will shine today no matter what. Fill your thoughts today of winning and the victory is yours. Step up step out and win win-win. Let's say it together I'm a winner win-win-win. Yes, winning sure does look good on you. Now smile and go be great. Love you and Peace

Gm Super Sunday. Today's energy must be on high because what you put out into the universe you are sure to get back. We are the energy of God so we must act in character, deeds, and ways of a god-like manner. Practice what you preach. Clean, clear, and pure thoughts of that which you desire. Dear God strengthens my actions and thoughts that I may manifest my dreams into my reality. I thank you for all my blessings. AMEN, AMEN, AMEN. Much love and Peace

Gm Meaningful Monday. I've been down, I've been hurt, I've been lost but through my God, I refuse to be broken. Even when we call it broken, we are not. When you say that you can't go on you can and will, when you are at that edge and you feel like you're going to fall off you're not. These are the reasons you need to awaken that godly spirit inside you. Through that source of power, we will continue. Dear God as you supply all my needs I humbly and graciously thank you. I thank you for giving me these understandings of your way and it is in your name we pray. AMEN, AMEN, AMEN. HAVE
AN OUTSTANDING DAY. RENDER LOVE NOT HATE, LOVE YOU, PEACE

Gm today is Talk too much Tuesday. I know you didn't want to hear that. Lol, We, often think we have a lot to say yet we don't have much to say at all. Instead of talking, I need you to listen and hear. You don't even sit down and listen to your own body. So today we are going to learn how to listen. You always calling on God to talk about what you need. Have you listened to his message, heard his messengers tell you what he needs from you. No, because you were too busy talking. Open your inner ear and eye to receive what is being said unto you. Sit and listen to someone today, you might hear the message God is sending for you. Dear God grant me the ability and patience to listen and hear. As you speak to me let me be able to draw that picture in my mind. Amen. Stop and listen don't say a word, God is telling you something. If you listening and hear me say AMEN, AMEN, AMEN. Have a loving day much love and respect. PEACE

Gm Wisdom Wednesday. With age and time, there should come wisdom and growth. Through trials and tribulations comes wisdom, not age and time. Time goes on and we may age but some stay 15, 20, or 30. They didn't understand their trials. As said on talk too much Tuesday (we don't listen nor do we hear). Today we will work it out for wisdom Wednesday. (CREATOR) [c] cultivating a [r] righteous reality [e] enduring, [a] achieving, and [t] teaching [o] our youth of their [r] righteous rewarding riches. Dear God, I give you the glory of my growth and change. I thank you for your blessings and mercy. AMEN, AMEN, AMEN. Go learn something today and grow love you. Peace

Gm TERRIFIC thinking Thursday. Some of us call today, throwback Thursday. Well, I got something for you to throw back. Throwback your bad thoughts, your disrespectful ways, your ungodly actions, the bad language, I can go on and on but you know what I'm saying. Let's replace it with positive thoughts, godly actions, caring and constructive words. We have to change the hearts and minds of each other today to something loving and caring. Dear God grabs hold of me and doesn't let go. I'm in a fight I can't win without you. Give me my roots back, allow me to grow beautiful minds and form them into creative hands and not destructive ones. It is forever in your hands God as we pray AMEN, AMEN, AMEN. Share a positive word today because you are beautiful. Love you and Peace

Gm Finding my way on this Freeway Friday. Today's message is dedicated to you wonderful WOMEN. I didn't say mother's because when you truly become a real woman your parental guidance and nurturing ways take over. I want to say thank you. Thank you for the continuous love, unconditional support, the tears of joy and pain, and the ways you teach your sons to treat women, and the way you teach your daughters to be women. We men can never thank you enough but we try. (I know I do always) men we must show them, protect them, and cherish them. Dear God, I thank you for these outstanding WOMEN, I ask that you continue to keep them and forever bless them. For they give the world the kindness it needs. AMEN, AMEN, AMEN. Mothers' day is every day. Love you and always know I'm going to make you proud of me. PEACE

Gm on this Satisfying Special Saturday. Again, today I want to give tribute to the WOMAN (MOTHER'S). First, any man that miss treats a woman can't love himself knowing that she was created from him for him.
    THANK YOU

I thank you for making sure I got here healthy and safe. Thank you for those long nights you lay beside me when I was sick or scared. Thank you for teaching me about love and sacrifice. Thank you for showing me how and what is respect. Thank you for that whooping you gave me to get me back in check. Yes, there is a long list of thanks that goes out to you mothers. A special hug to those whose mother isn't physically here with us but know she is forever in our hearts. Dear God as you ease my pain fill my spirit with your love. I can never thank you enough for the countless blessings you have given us. I just want to be a blessing to others as you are to me. I ask that you send your motherly angels out to blanket the world with their love. AMEN, AMEN, AMEN. Women are blessed today and always and know I love you. PEACE

Gm Super Sunday. Happy mothers' day. As we take today to acknowledge the lifelong contribution that you wonderful WOMEN have given to humanity, I am truly thankful and blessed to have you in my life. You all have in some shape form or fashion contributed to my raising into a man. So, men, I hope you are listening give thanks today to that woman in your world that makes your life special. Dear God in your amazing works I say thank you for your most sacred gift (WOMAN). Allow them to stand strong and strive in your footsteps. AMEN, AMEN, AMEN. How lucky we are because of you. Have a blessed and loved-filled day. love you and thanks. PEACE

Gm Meaningful Monday. As we look back on yesterday being mothers' day, I'll say to you (sons and daughters) also to the (men) our mothers and women PERIOD should be given the utmost respect and protection. They deserve our devotion towards their happiness. From this day forward if you have not, make it your duty to show them their honor. Dear God forever reminds me of the joy you have given the world when you created the woman. They show the true lifeline to heaven. Thank you for all your blessings. AMEN, AMEN, AMEN. Every day say thank you to a woman because she has shown you what love and sacrifice are. WOMEN STAND UP AS WE MEN BOW DOWN TO GIVE YOU HONOR. Stay blessed love you and Peace.

Good evening talk about it Tuesday. time to stop talking and doing. Lots of us say a lot and do nothing. Let's put up or shut up. Men I'm calling on you to stand up for God and take care of your family. Teach your young men how and what it is to be a man, not a male. Women I need you to show these Lil girls what a woman is and want a best friend in your child but the best image of yourself in your child. God gave you the tools to multiply and cultivate. You have been multiplying now begin to cultivate. Teach our children something other than looking cute. Dear God help me save our youth and parents give me the knowledge to do your work. AMEN, AMEN, AMEN. Have a great evening and Peace

Gm Where do I go Wednesday? On this journey where will you go? I realize that I'm different. I'm not the same as I once was. The older you get the more you should grow mentally, emotionally, economically, and spiritually. You grow in this urge to be closely connected to your God. Once you allow that connection to form a whole new world begins. The fight becomes real. You see things you overlooked things take a different meaning. We are forever trying to find our purpose in life moving around from one thing to the next. Today we are building a foundation that will continue to give you directions to a better life. Dear God as you grow my roots in this foundation, I thank you for being my strength and guide. Without you none of whom I'll become is possible. It is you that is owned by my faithfulness. AMEN, AMEN, AMEN. Let God take you where you need to be, give him the chance that you have given others, and know he won't let you down. In the words of a great person (GOD GOT ME (YOU) PEACE.

Gm Take me Thursday. I am sick, you are sick, we all are sick and in need of healing. Every day we sit and see our people's lives being destroyed by their sickness. The lack of spirituality, lack of self-love, lack of knowledge, lack of direction plagues our cities all over the world. Is there a cure for stupidity, a cure for hate, a cure for evilness? YES, there is and that cure is God. Dear God I come to you today asking that you take me. Take us God and cure us of this sickness we have. Only you can cure these inflictions. AMEN, AMEN, AMEN. Yes, we are sick now who is with me going to God for help. Have an awesome day much love and Peace.

Gm Freedom of speech Friday. On this freeway journey, we want to talk about freedom of speech. Here is my freedom of speech. (_____

_____

_____) Yes, that's me being quiet, I'm listening to God speak. When you listen to God there is nothing to be said. As I listen to God and he directs me to speak then I know I have something good to say. It should be quiet where you are also if you all are listening to God. Remember the saying if you don't have anything good to say don't say anything. (Me whispering) it should be very quiet where you are or very loud because you all are praising God. Dear God as you allow these words to flow out my mouth blesses the ears that are listening to them. Allow them to speak your words to your people. AMEN, AMEN, AMEN. Words are powerful and hurtful once spoken they can't be taken back. Speak words of a KING or QUEEN, speak words of a true MOTHER or FATHER, SPEAK THE WORDS OF GOD, BUT FIRST LISTEN TO A KING, QUEEN, MOTHER, FATHER, AND MOST OF ALL LISTEN AND PAY ATTENTION TO THE WORDS OF GOD. I LOVE YOU AND HAVE A LISTENING DAY. PEACE.

Gm Satisfying Saturday. Dear God today is a beautiful day and I thank you for it. I thank you for the peace that you have put into my life, I thank you for the love you surround me with. I ask that you continue to give me the strength and allow your words to flow through me. AMEN, AMEN, AMEN. We often talk about hate well let's look at it. (HATE) a word that stresses a strong dislike for something. Ok, first you must know something about the thing which you hate and most time we know nothing. We hate just because. Crazy right. Well, I want you to learn about the thing that you hate before you take that stance. With some of our ugly ways, God should hate us but he doesn't. Love you Peace Gm Super Sunday. Yes, God keeps sending blessings my way all through the night and all through the day God keeps sending blessings my way. Dear God I come to you for healing. I ask of you to give healing to these wicked minds of your children. AMEN, AMEN, AMEN. Let's have some church, God sends blessings often. He allows doors The basics and pathways to open for you when you think there is no hope. Then we reply (won't he do it). Then there are times when God's wrath must come down. When his people are not following his way. Some of us say his wrath is our karma. The universal law of cause and effect. Our punishment for our disobedience to God was to fall from grace and even then, he still gave us dominion over everything. He also gave us a pathway back to grace. I ask that you join me on that journey getting back in God's great grace. All through the night and all through the day we are on the pathway back to grace with God. Come walk with me. Have a blessed Sunday and love you Peace

Gm Mending Monday. As we continue with making meaning of things, we come to mending Monday. Being broken is so hard to admit that we begin to forge a lie in our mind that we are ok for so long that the broken part begins to feel natural. Well, no more, it's time to take that broken part of you to the shop of God and let him fix it. Let go and let God do the healing for you. Man/woman can't always fix what's wrong in your world only God can. We don't always have to be strong sometimes we need to let out a good cry. We all need a shoulder to lean on sometimes. Dear God I come to you yet again broken and disappointed with the ways of the world, I ask that you please step in and fix it. Give me the knowledge and directions to heal your children and your children's children. I thank you. AMEN, AMEN, AMEN. You're not alone call me, I and God will listen. Have a blessed day Peace.

Gm Take your place Tuesday. Today we got kids acting like they are the parent and parents acting like they are the child. Men, it's time for you to be that man you say you are. Take responsibility for your life. Women are the nurturing woman you should be. You're mothering that child from the womb to the grave. We have lost our place in this world. Even with knowing God. There is so much to learn about God. Dear God, please put us in the place where we belong. Give us the knowledge to be the best parents we can be, the greatest understanding, and the ability to be the best children we can be. Also, give us your guidance to be the best servant for you we can be. AMEN, AMEN, AMEN. As we all take our place in life let it be a place of good and love. Today give a hug we all need one. Have a God-filled day Peace. love you.

Good evening, we all we go Wednesday. This saying is well misunderstood. At one time we relied on one another and we could depend on each other. Now if it's not for again we let each other down a no cost. Let make the saying true again (we all we got). Hey, you yes you, I know you got me just like I know God got us. Dear God, you are all we got and we going to be all you need to get our people back in line. Have a good evening much love Peace.

Gm take your time Thursday. As we trust in God, ask him to give you the patience to take your time and enjoy the life he has given you. The world is in such a rush and for what. I want you to stop and take a look around you and just look. Things could be worse but it's not. We must be more appreciative of what we have. I have life, love, and laughter. Dear God thank you for the things you provide for me every day. Through you, I am victorious all day every day. Thank you. Amen. God bless you and enjoy life. Peace

Gm full of joy Friday. Joy-joy. We allow people and things to come into our lives and just steal away our joy. Sadden us, confuse us, stress us, and then we sit around and let ourselves down. STOP get off that ride, get rid of whatever it is that is taking away your joy. Peace has no price so we all should be at peace and full of joy. Dear God restore the joy and peace in our world. Allow them to see that there is joy in having a life. I pray the joy back in your life. AMEN, AMEN, AMEN let nothing steal your joy. Be joyful and peaceful today and always. Lots of love Peace

Gm Soul Searching Saturday. On this Satisfying day let's do some soul searching. What do you feel deep down inside your soul about yourself? Yes, your poop stink too. We don't like to deal with ourselves and I use to wonder why. Until I had to, only deal with myself. When you can self-evaluate and self-motivate then you see how much self-

improvement you need. So now as we work on you for others can see you for who you truly are not for the role you are auditioning for. There is three-part of you (the person you were, the person you are, then the person you want to be). The truth is always somewhere in the middle. Lol. As you read this next part replace the words that fit you. (I AM A STRONG BLACK MAN/WOMAN, I AM A MAN/WOMAN OF RESPECT AND CHARACTER, I AM BEAUTIFUL AND INTELLIGENT YES THAT'S ME A CHILD OF GOD). Dear God give me the strength to live up to the highest quality of your standards and forever remain humble. AMEN, AMEN, AMEN. Hey KING/QUEEN God is watching let's give Him an amazing show. Go be awesome in all that you do in the name of God.
Much love and respect Peace

Gm Super Sunday. Today is about thanks. Dear God, I thank you for this blessed day. AMEN. Be thankful today, say thank you to those that have never strayed from your corner. Look around you and be ever grateful that you have a roof over your head, food to eat, and someone you can call when needed. I thank you yes you and I'm ever so thankful to God for keeping me when I needed him most. Have a thankful day and much love. PEACE

Gm Meaningful Monday. FAITH is a strong belief in something or someone. Having a strong foundation belief system in a higher power (GOD). Even without knowledge or understanding, we know something far beyond us created everything we see before us. What makes the sunrise and set? What makes the many different bodies of water flow? What changes the different climates we feel? Questions as a child we ask. As we grow, we grow in understanding and knowledge which then reveals to us (God). No matter what happens in life we know God is the beginning and the ending. To gain clarity of things in life go to God at the beginning and thank him in the end. Dear God continue to bless us as we grow in life, never release us from our life sentence with you. AMEN, AMEN. Be gone evil you can't have us we are God's children. Be faithful to God and do his work. Have a blessed day   you and Peace

Gm Time Ticking Tuesday. As time passes on, we scramble around in a hurry to get things done. We are only focused on time, not the task. We are always in a rush and why. Are we in such a rush because we know tomorrow is not a promise or are we just not wanting to do what's at hand? Well, make time, have time, and take your time for yourself and God. Slow down you are going to miss this beautiful life being in a rush. Dear God, I thank you for the time you have invested in me, for the time you took in creating me. I am forever grateful that you are always on time, in time, and have time for me. AMEN, AMEN, AMEN. Know that time is precious but don't lose time being in a rush. Have a blessed and wonderful day. Peace

Gm afternoon on this Where do we go Wednesday. As always, we are working things out in our self and our lives, so I ask where do we go? I'm going where my positive thoughts and road can take me. Some say we were born into sin I say we were born out of sin and as we left the stage of pureness as a baby we went back into sin with our ways and actions. Now as we move back and forward from trying to be sin-free we fail at times.

Keep your faith, stay strong, and believe in yourself. The path to take is in front of you, gear up let's ride. Have a great day Peace much love.

Gm Turn around Thursday. Today I want to say to our PRESENT PAST AND FUTURE MOTHER'S. You will always be precious, protected, and provided for. So, as I speak to the SONS and DAUGHTERS of these mother's I say to them listen and hear me. (As you carried me to your birth date you did your best that no harm came to me, from my first breath, my first step, the losing of my first tooth you were there, my first girl/boyfriend to my husband/wife or my BFF for life, you been there when I finally got my heartbroken you were there. I can never repay you for the pain that I may have caused but I know I will forever do my best at showing you I love you and making you proud of me.) We often take things for granted unintentionally because we are so distracted by our things. No more disrespect, no more I'm busy, give them their love and respect today. Turn this around our women are unique and highly favored by a God that we need to learn about. I say to you lovely women HAPPY WOMAN'S DAY. Dear God as you have given man his second most precious gift (woman) we thank you and we will honor you by protecting them and respecting them. AMEN. Women are beautiful as always and men show them, they are appreciated. Much love Peace

Gm Focus Friday. There are many distractions in the world and being focused is a must. Staying on a positive path I find is a challenging thing. Surrounding yourself with like-minded people and having constructive habits can help with focusing. Every damaging trigger that we have is challenged when we are doing the right things in life. The devil is hard at work doing all that's possible to pull you off that path. Remember you first must allow the devil the opportunity to get you off your path so learn to stay clear of these triggers. Dear God keep me focused and grounded in my strength to do my best. Amen. Have a great day and keep your eyes open, ears listening, and mouth closed. PEACE

Gm Survivor Saturday. We are survivors of many life setbacks. Yes, we made it through many storms that have left physical, mental, emotional, and spiritual scars upon us that show our battles and pain. Yet we ask (why me God?) And I say why not you. Aren't you made for God's trials and tribulations? This molds you into what we call a woman/man. This humbles you into a life of peace and happiness. When you have truly looked misery in the face you know there is a great God that is fighting with you. You are a survivor of all you thought would or could break you. Look at you shining right now. Standing with your head held up high, feeling good about yourself. Let it be known you are a Survivor. Dear God thank you for your shield and armor that got me to the other side where there is peace around me. Thank you for protecting me in my fight with myself. AMEN, AMEN, AMEN. If no one has told you (I'm very proud of you and love you, survivor). Be blessed Peace

Gm Super Sunday. Y'all ready for Church. How do we know when God is speaking? (You) you don't know because you not listening. You are tuned in to a different channel. God speaks to Man through MAN. God said you need to be on the frequency or station that he is broadcasting on. When a man speaks you have to be careful, you don't know who is talking, is it The Man, a man, or the other man. The Man is God coming through you to render help to his people, a man is that unconscious fool inside you, and the other man is that devil trying to get you to poison the people. I know God is real for what he has done with me, for me, and around me. He closed my mouth and tuned my ears to hear him speak and when he is ready for me to talk, he gives me words of joy, peace, and love to share. Let me say that again. When he wants me to speak, he gives me words of joy, peace, and love to share, are you listening to God? We need to tune into God every day all day. Today God is talking, he is pouring raindrops of love down upon us to wash away the dirt and hate in the air. Dear God, we come to you today thanking you for your mercy. Thank you for keeping us safe. AMEN, AMEN, AMEN. In the words of a great and wonderful friend (GOD GOT ME (US) IM (WE) GOOD) HAVE AN OUTSTANDING DAY MUCH LOVE PEACE

Gm Memory Monday. Our memory doesn't fail us we just fail to remember. We got what people call selective memory. You don't recall that ignorant stuff you did last week. You don't remember God sparing your life. You can't quite recall all the lies you told. Yet you remember the little amount of good you've done. Well, let me help you clear up some things. When you were down and out God opened some doors for you to help you make a way. When you thought you just couldn't go on living God put you on his back and carried you until you could stand on your own two feet. When you didn't believe in yourself God showed you that you are a winner and believed in you. See your memory might be short but God's blessings for you have been never-ending. So, the very next time you get selective memory look up, look around, and you will see that God has been reaching

out for you always. Don't let your memory fail you again because then you will fail to get or receive your blessings. Have a remember all day love you. Peace

Chapter 6

June

June words for June...

JUSTICE = JUSTICE LIVES IN THE JUST.

**UNDERSTANDING = COMMUNICATION BRINGS
UNDERSTANDING**

NOTICE = WE WERE PUT ON NOTICE AT BIRTH

**EVERLASTING = WITH GOD IS WHERE
EVERLASTING LIFE RESIDES**

Gm Turn around Tuesday. Turn around and face me. Stop walking past the mirror and not looking at me. I am you and you are me now turn around and face me (you). You can't do anything without me and I can't go anywhere without you so stop avoiding me. Yes, I'm the man/woman in the mirror. Facing yourself is hard but know that it's worth it once you do. Dear God help us face ourselves. God, we are ready for your change. We thank you for your guidance. AMEN. You are beautiful, you are intelligent, you are strong now turn around and look at yourself. Be blessed love you Peace.

Good evening won't he do it Wednesday? We know that God will come through for us now will you come through for God and yourself. See when you're getting yourself right you working for God. Now when you don't want to put that time in on self then you working for the other team. Are we always yelling who are you with? God wants to know who are you with. Get your life in order just like that. Times are changing out here and it's time to get on the good train or get left behind. Who are you with? Well, I pray that you all had a great day and I wish you a wonderful evening. Y'all get on board now you hear. Love you and Peace oh, I'm with God.

Good evening throw it back Thursday. Reality check for those that have no respect for the elderly and the children of young ages. From a baby, you come and a baby you shall return. Your parent took care of you and provided for you as a child so as they grow old and need you to take care of them do so because your turn will come back around for your children to take care of you. God said honor they father and mother and your

days will belong on this earth land. Be
good children and outstanding parents.
Throw this one back to your fan club.
Have a blessed evening Peace love you.

Gm Front line Friday. What is it that
mentally we gravitate to the rear of the
room, bus, plane, etc. It's like we have
been taught this pattern through (his-
story). Well, it's time to be upfront.
Upfront with everything no longer taking
a back seat nor left behind. You are born
leaders so to lead you are out front. Get
out of the shadows we need you to take
control of our lives and our children's
lives things around us are far out of
hand. We are in the back videoing
everything. Dear God protect them that's
out front making a change, give the ones
in the back the strength to come upfront.
AMEN. Stand up worrier of God and
come out front.
Peace and much love.

Gm Searching Saturday. Yes, as children we search out answers to everything we come in contact with. As adults (parents) we are to give answers to that which our children seek answers. Now as adults we search out stability, security, and understanding to the mess we have made of parts of our lives. Many of us will do what it takes to make the changes needed and others will continue to place the blame on others. This is why at some point in our early age we need to be searching for God. From a child, our inquisitive minds search for answers as young adults we need to search and find a spiritual foundation. Dear God give me the answers to my questions. Place in my Google maps the directions to you. AMEN, AMEN, AMEN. Love you to health in your search of your God. PEACE.

Gm Start me up Sunday. Dear God I want to thank you for getting my life started today, I want to thank you for the many blessings that you have given me continuously. You have always given me the best of you and I must do much better at giving you the best of me. AMEN, AMEN, AMEN.

Start your day knowing that all things will go as planned.

Tell yourself that nothing will stop your progress in life. Whatever you want to call your setbacks you may, just don't call it quits. Winners never give up and quitters never win. King and Queen stand up you have a village to control. Be encouraged today and always. Love you Peace.

Gm Mam up Monday. Yes, it's time to man up around here. You say that you are grown men/women when really you are some grown boys/girls. You're acting like you don't see the problems or you just want to sidestep everything. Well, you weren't raised that way so it's time to man up. Oops, I said all that when some of us don't even know what a real MAN/WOMAN is. Well, we are in the business of growing real men and women. Take a moment and have this conversation with your parents and parents ask your parents (what is a real man/woman)? These topics are not being talked about in homes today. Get it back in order. Man up! Man up! Dear God don't send me out into this world disobedient and lost, help me gain the knowledge and understanding of what a man/woman of God should be. AMEN, AMEN, AMEN. Be great let's love each other. PEACE.

Gm Tuesday! Dear God, I thank you for another day to be the best I can be in your eyesight. I thank you for all your blessings. AMEN. Today we still focusing on manning up.

There is a shortage of men/women in this world. Not many want to be responsible. Have a great day much love Peace.

Good evening where did the time go Wednesday? We often think time is on our side well it's not. Time waits for no one. If you are not moving with time, in time, and on time you will be left behind. Stop sitting around doing nothing thinking that God is going to send the answers to your prayers on the couch. Dear God as we prepare to rest for the night. I thank you for the quiet time. I look forward to you waking me in the morning time. Peace, have a great and peaceful night.

Gm Teach me something new Thursday. There is a saying that says (there is nothing new under the sun) well maybe not but if you haven't experienced it, it's new to you. Lol. Growing is about seeing and learning new things. Like this word (Trichoptilosis) who knows what this means? Well, it's split ends of the hair. You learned something. Continue to grow and learn it's a lot in this world we don't know. Dear God, I thank you for this day along with the blessings and lessons I will receive. AMEN. Have a learning day love you Peace.

Good evening family and friends. This is about family and friends Friday. What is life without family and life not fun without a friend? Today your friends are more like family and your family just blood-related. Got to remember Cain killed Abel, and now all you see is black brothers killing another black brother. We need to get it together family and friends. Dear God, we are seeking your guidance and help for we are suffering at a rapid pace. Reach out and touch the souls of our lost youth and our miss understood parents. AMEN, AMEN, AMEN. I pray that you all evening will be joyful and blessed. PEACE.

Hey everyone I missed yesterday. Silent Saturday. At times we need to just be quiet and hear what's going on around us and with us. Be silent enough to hear your own heartbeat. You may find out that your flow is off. Everything we do at times is so noisy and messy. So, let us be very quiet Peace.
Good afternoon super Sunday. God-God- God- God- God and more God. have a godly day. Peace.

Good evening MENs Monday. You are not a father, you are not a parent, you are not a dad, you are not responsible, you just may be the sperm donor.

Fathers -day is coming and the children have been looking for you since August and now you want to be recognized. Man up and be a constant in your child's or children's lives. They need us, men, to step up and help guide these children on a great path. Calling all men can you please stand up and be counted on and for. By the way, women if you are acting as both mother and father, I congratulate you on a job well done. Dear God put the KING back in these fallen men. AMEN, AMEN, AMEN. Have a blessed day and Peace love you.

Gm Tough love Tuesday. Yes, tough love. See tough love is telling you the truth no matter what, not telling you what you want to hear. Tough love is being on your side good or bad, tough love is loving someone through the pain. Tough love doesn't walk nor run away when things not going their way. We are so used to conditional love that tough and real love never gets a chance. So, we need to get away from the conditional situation and get into a real and tough situation. Dear God thank you for your real tough love. Thank you for never walking away from me. Thank you for believing in me. AMEN, AMEN, AMEN. Have a real and tough-loving kind of day. Peace love you!!!!!!!!!!!!!!

Good evening Where are the Men at Wednesday? We look around and we see a great number of MALES around but are they being real men. There is a shortage of REAL (fathers, brothers, uncles, friends) of the male population. See our concept of real is incorrectly used. Now once again I'm calling on all MEN to step up and lead their household. We need the man structure in them. Not just a body because anybody can fill that role. We need FULL-TIME male (MEN) role models in our cities. Dear God empowers our males with the guidance needed to lead our youth to a better life. AMEN, AMEN, AMEN. Have a wonderful and blessed night Peace love you.

Gm Telling the Truth Thursday. God is good all the time. Won't he do it every day? He never leaves my side. God has a purpose for me. Action speaks louder than words. These are truths. The thing we can count on once we put it into practice (God laws). Man law is to suit his Inability to stay on the right path. Man's law gives you an excuse to do stupid stuff and wrong. Now God's law empowers you to constantly do better and grow. Dear God, we thank you for your mercy and love. We thank you for each and every day. AMEN, AMEN, AMEN. Tell your truths today, have an amazing day, and be blessed. Love you Peace.

Good evening, Fathering Friday. I congratulate you father's that is doing all that is needed to prepare your children for the life ahead of them. You mother's that is acting in both roles are the same to you as well. It is a must that we stay the course with raising our children. Just because they become of age that they say they are grown our guidance is still needed. We often push them out the nest and they are not prepared for what they will be facing. Continue to love and be there for your children. Dear God continues to give your love as we share your love with others. AMEN, AMEN, AMEN. Have a great evening and much love Peace.

Good afternoon Shaping up Saturday. Everybody getting their body fit and tight. It's hot time to look sexy and cute women, and men want to be buff and ripped. That's right get it in. Now, what happens when the question on your text asks? (where was the first black wall street) or (what is the human body made of) some will draw a blank because they are so caught up on the outer that the brain and spirit suffer. Things in life have its (time, place, and reason). We need structure and guidance. Yes, we also want to look fabulous but don't leave out the rest of you in the process. Be blessed and have a fit kind of day. Peace.

Gm Saving Sunday. God is in the business of saving lives you just have to go to his office for your physical therapy. To all the father's I want you to know that today is just a small token of who you are and what you mean to your children. You are needed in all these families. So, as you enjoy this father's -day know we love you for what you do. Happy father's-day. Dear God as you strengthen these father's guide them into being outstanding parents. Protect them as they protect and provide for their families. AMEN, AMEN, AMEN! Go to God He saves lives. Have a blessed and amazing day Peace. Love you.

Good evening on this Meaningful Monday. Yesterday we celebrated father's- day we'll men know this being a father is the same as being a mother 365 days a year you are a father. So don't walk away with a day of honor and start tripping till next year. Stay the course it really takes a village to raise a family and the King is needed. If you call yourself a man represents. It's time for men to get in the game. Dear God continues to strengthen our men to step up and be kings. AMEN, AMEN, AMEN Have a great evening Peace.

Good afternoon on this Try me Tuesday.
(In God we trust) is printed on the dollar
bill, but do we trust God or the dollar. We
are so hungry for a dollar but on a 30 day
fast from God. We make all kinds of
preparations to eat but nothing for the
spirit and soul. Stop putting materials in
front of our existence. Dear God, I put
you first just as you have done me. I
thank you for every day and blessings.
AMEN, AMEN, AMEN. Continue to enjoy
the rest of your day Peace love you.

Goodnight whispering Wednesday.
Talking low as a whisper doesn't mean
you're afraid it means once your voice is
raised things will get very different.
Talking low shows your control of
yourself. Loud is a sign of an out-of-
control person. Dear God give me
calmness and control. AMEN, AMEN,

AMEN. Have a great night much love. Peace.

Good afternoon Time heals all things Thursday. Yes, in time things get better. You first must give it time to get better. We have what we call (right now syndrome). Life doesn't beat to just your drum. There is more to life than just you, yours, and yourself. There is an us, them and theirs. Give life a chance and you will enjoy it. Dear God allow us the time to enjoy all your blessings. AMEN, AMEN, AMEN. Have a wonderful rest of your day Peace.

Gm Freeway Friday. Yes, back on the road again. This road
TRIP will really get you thinking. On this trip, I'm taking (imagination, insight, hindsight, subconscious, curiosity, and spirit) See these things within you function together. They relay messages

and images to each other so that we can survive

Good evening, Freeway Friday. Back on the road. This ride I'm riding with imagination, consciousness, subconscious, hindsight, curiosity, and spirit. These personal traits allow you to fully function. Each one serves a unique purpose within yourself. So, if you understand then some don't. I suggest that you get to know them. Each one gives the other information that the other needs. Get to know yourself in all areas. Have a blessed night Peace love you.

Good evening Standing still Saturday. Yes, you are standing still stuck in one place or time because you refuse to expand your understanding. Things have to be your way or no way. Therefore, nowhere is where you get. We must come to terms with the fact (we don't know it all) in fact sometimes we don't know jack... Universal laws indicate that we need each other to move ahead. Dear God give me the understanding to know when I'm stuck in one place or time. AMEN, AMEN, AMEN Have a blessed evening Peace.

Good afternoon on Super Sunday. Ready for some praising. Giving the all-mighty God all the glory and praise for getting us here. Gathering all our strength and power from you God. We are ever more grateful for your mercy. We all need to know to put God first in all that we do. What you accomplish in life it's 99.9 % God and .1% you. Dear God, we thank you for always getting us where we need to be. AMEN, AMEN, AMEN. Have a super day you super people. Peace.

Good afternoon on this Managing Monday. Some things in our lives need to be managed. We tend to over-do quite a bit of things. We need to pause and regroup. Things in our life can take more energy out of us than we expected. Once this happens it often is replaced with bad energy because we are now frustrated and have had enough. So, let us take the time to manage things properly. Dear God help me manage my life. AMEN, AMEN, AMEN. Have the best evening possible Peace.

Great night. This Tell me something good Tuesday. In this late hour I only come to say (I see you) I see your work, I see your blessings, I see your mercy. Now it's time for you to see me share your love. How many of you can say (I'm here if you need me) my ears and heart is open to you. God sent me to offer you his guidance and directions. He said there is but one way to him and that is of truth and faith. Dear God watch over us

as we sleep and wake us to a greater day.
AMEN, AMEN, AMEN Have a blessed night Peace.
Good afternoon, won't he do it Wednesday? I want to give a special shout-out to the Men that have continued to stand up and handle their responsibilities as a man should. I'm proud of you guys for remaining strong. Women I want to thank you all for giving us men a chance to show that we are worthy. You may be the foundation but we are the strength that is needed to hold it together. Dear God thank you for

continuing your work on us. AMEN, AMEN, AMEN. Have a blessed day. Peace! Today say to someone (won't he do it) because God knows we all are trying. Xoxo

Chapter 7

July

July is the month of Americans Independence. Yet we are so dependent on something.

JUDGEMENTAL = WE ARE SO JUDGEMENTAL OF OTHERS CHOICES.

UNCONDITIONAL = WE ARE ALWAYS PLACING CONDITIONS ON OTHERS.

LOVE = LOVE TRUTHFULLY AND IT WILL BE RETURNED

YOU = EVERYTHING ALWAYS STARTS WITH YOU.

Gm Touch of class Thursday. Women you are unique and different. You have a level of style and class that reaches past most imagination. when some of you step out you really show out others show off which is not classy. Men you have a swag that come from generations of dignity and vigor. Men we wanted to be known for being the flyist on the scene. Men and women get your class back show off your mind and brilliance. An intelligent mind is the most attractive thing in the world then put a heart of spirituality on top of it and you are awesome. Dear God help us get our class back. AMEN, AMEN, AMEN. Have a blessed day and Peace. Forming Friday. Forming Friday is about shaping your life.

Shaping it into something meaningful. Don't just live, (explore) build a legacy a brand that your children's children can have.

Standing still Saturday. No longer are we standing in one place. Some of us only know the distance from our house to the Conner store. We are standing still afraid to explore, don't want to take a chance and see the opportunities in the world.

Searching Sunday. We are on a search each and every day. Looking for something. Some are looking for gossip, some are looking for drama, some are looking for love, we all need to be looking for God. Instead of googling the latest dance google directions to God. Let's see if you can follow these instructions. I've searched my whole life for what was right in front of me, I just didn't know who I was. I finally found myself. Thanks to my strength in God, he opened my eyes up to be able to see myself. Dear God give us all the strength to search for you and ourselves. I have searched high and low and nothing can compare to what I've found in God. You all have a blessed and fun finding day Peace!

Good evening Making it happen Monday. Yes, it is time to make things happen. Sitting around doesn't get results, getting up and working and moving towards what you want will get results. We have sat around long enough now we need to come together and grow. Dear God give us the direction and courage to get up and make things happen for our life to be better, AMEN, AMEN Have a great evening Peace.

Good evening turn your life around Tuesday. Guidance and directions are very important in our lives today. (Where do I get my guidance from?) Your first voice comes while you are being carried for 9 months. That voice speaks to you in a soft and oh so gentle voice. Telling you how much they are going to love you and give you the world. (Mother) Then you come into this world of confusion. Wow Yet that strong mother still gives you what she can to raise you right. Then you go and get world slick trying all kinds of things. Then you go running back to momma for help. I want to give all of you strong, forever supportive, and always a loving mother's a well-needed THANKS. You are and always will be the best. Then you come to meet God and here is where your direction will come from. Dear God thank you for your direction. AMEN, AMEN, AMEN. Have a great evening Peace.

Gm Will power Wednesday. Our willpower has to be strong to help us make it through some difficult times. Mental strength is needed today and always. God give us the strength to

make it through. AMEN, AMEN, AMEN!
Have an awesome day Peace.

Gm testimony Thursday. Everyone has a
story to tell. A rough road traveled a
hardship to share that will chill a soul.
Different from each other but the same in
one unique way.
Each of us can stand today and say
THANKS TO GOD AND ONLY GOD, I
MADE IT THROUGH IT ALL. I've hurt so
many nights but he got me up in the
morning and said stand my child stand.
Dear God thank you for keeping me lifted
and gifted. AMEN, AMEN, AMEN. As you
face life challenges and changes know
God is there always. I'm also here much
love and Peace. Be great today and
blessed

Good evening Full of life Friday. Let no
one steal your joy in life. No matter who
it is your joy and peace are more

important. God gave me my peace and my love of life is my joy. Dear God thank you for my peace and for granting me my joy each and every day. AMEN, AMEN, AMEN. Bath in your peace and dance with your joy you deserve to be happy. Have a great evening Peace.

Gm STAND, STRIVE, SILENCE, SURRENDER SATURDAY. Sit and Silence yourself so that you can hear God talking to you. Surrender yourself to God he is your answer and provider. Stand up and be counted for and counted on. Know that you are worthy and needed. Strive for greatness in all that you do. You have an audience watching to see you fail prove them wrong show them your God is great. Dear God thank you for your mercy and love. AMEN, AMEN, AMEN. If you haven't been told know this (I appreciate you, I believe in you, I am proud of you.) Have an awesome day Peace.

Gm Sightseeing Sunday. Yes, we are sightseeing all the time. Window shopping, club-hopping, gossip finding, etc. Why is it so hard for us to focus on something and move towards it the world has so many distractions that it keeps us from obtaining the goals we set out to do in life? Dear God please keep me focused on the right and positive things in life. AMEN, AMEN Have a beautiful Sun fun day. Peace!

Gm Making mistakes Monday. Years ago, when I was growing up, we would make a mistake and we would APOLOGIZE AND CORRECT it. Today people make mistakes
and say (ow well, it ain't that serious, let it go) well it isn't ow well, and it is that serious, and I won't just get over it. Take

responsibility for your actions today, be thoughtful of others' feelings, be mindful that there are consequences for your actions. Today's children have lost or were never taught RESPECT. We talk about whooping these kids we need to whoop some parents also. As God continues to watch over you have a blessed day correcting your mistakes. PEACE, love you to correctness.

Great night teaching Tuesday. Life is all about learning. As we grow in size and age it's all a learning experience. So, as we meet people, we teach people. Be sure to teach all positive things. Peace!

Great night on this Where am I going Wednesday. Lost, confused, and troubled with choices and directions. Often times we think we going crazy this is when we need to slow it down and ask ourselves (where are you taking me).

Don't be in such a rush and make mistake Monday keep repeating itself. Focus and ask God. Have a blessed night Peace.

Good evening, Tribute Thursday. We often let people in our life go unacknowledged. We check on them when we hear they are sick or broke down and dying. Well, I'm here to acknowledge you now while you're strong and vibrant. Hey you, I see you, I'm proud of you. Thank you for being a real friend, brother, sister etc. Let me see you smile because you are loved not only by me but by God. Enjoy your evening Peace.

Good evening Finding peace Friday. When life has taken you for a long ride of pain, disappointment, and anger finding peace is the greatest gift to find. Having peace doesn't cost a penny but is worth thousands. Dear God help me find peace in this chaotic world. AMEN, AMEN. Have a peaceful night. Much love and Peace.

Gm Staying in contact with God Saturday. Ok yes, I said it (staying in contact with God). We call on God when things get rough, we in pain, trouble hits your front door. Why weren't you praising him when you got that good job, hit that number, found the love of your life. God should be at the top of the list for every category. No matter what the issue is we should (thank you God, help me God, I'm grateful God). Not only when things not going well, but we also need God all the time. Thanks to him we are here. So today tune into your God station and stay connected. Much love and Peace. By the way, how are you today?

Good evening Speaking up Sunday. Speak up for right speak out about wrong. We have been promoting wrong so long that speaking up for right feels wrong for some. It's time to get things back in order. Stop letting them think that it's cool to do wrong to anyone. Dear God bring us together for right give us the strength to speak out about wrong. God help me be better at doing right myself. AMEN, AMEN, AMEN You all speak up and have a great evening Peace love

Gm Monday. I want you to give thought to this subject here. Today we walk pass each other and don't even speak. (Say gm, hello, or greetings). We walk around like no one exists but us. People, we are not alone in this world start showing some concern for others. You don't have to know me to say GM. Then again some of us don't even say GM and thank you to God for waking us up. Dear God thank you for this day. AMEN, AMEN, AMEN.

Check-in on your family and loved ones let them know that they matter. PEACE.

Good evening, Thunderstorm Tuesday. When you hear the thunder, you know there is a storm coming. Rain, winds, and lightning cause all kinds of chaos. Grandma would tell be quiet and stay still to respect God he is working things out also. After the storm there is peace. We often have to go through a storm to find our peace. Stay focused and prayed up Peace much love.

Good evening, Word misrepresentation Wednesday. We often say things just to be heard saying something slick. (Love you dog, my nigga, I got you, etc). Stop giving people false hope of your fake words of concern. We have to get back to where once we said it it was law. We meant every word. If we meant these words our society would not be in so much pain and hurt. Say what you mean and mean what you say. Dear God I pray for peace and protection of our children. AMEN, AMEN, AMEN. Have a great evening meaning what you say Peace much love.

Good night, Trouble doesn't last long Thursday. Trouble only lasts as long as you will allow it. Once you speak peace into existence then trouble leave the scene. Now if you sit in your trouble then pack your lunch it will be around for a while. You have the power to control your situations. Never give power to others give power to God and God alone. Have a trouble-free night and may God watch over you and yours as you sleep. Peace and love.

Good night, FINDING FAITH FRIDAY. Finding faith is finding the strength within yourself to make it through all obstacles in your way of success. Success is yours just believe and ask God for your direction and it's waiting for you. Have a great and peaceful night. PEACE.

Goodnight Something on my mind Saturday. When people have things on their minds it can rip them apart, others will grow and become stronger. We are to think and contemplate our ideas. Our minds only grow as we feed it. What are you feeding your mind Feed it something spiritual, something wholesome, something that will expand it not destroy it? Have a great and healthy night. Much love and Peace.

Good morning Super Sunday, today it is all about worship.
We are going to PRAY AND PRAY.
Have a great day peace.

Good evening, My name got Meaning Monday. Your parents named you and in their minds, at the time your name is to represent something. Not your last name but your given name. I was named after an angel and I know my mom search her head every day wondering what was wrong when I was a child. Well, you grow into the meaning of your name. Just as we all have a purpose in life the meaning of our name stands for something. Find out what yours stand for. Be blessed and happy finding. PEACE.

Gm Take control Tuesday. Taking control means looking in the mirror and fixing what's going on with you first. Once that has been done, we can go out in the community and help with what's going on there. Our community needs healing very badly. We look for peace but how many of you have given peace to your community. We walk pass each other and won't even speak. Let's get it together. Too much drama in our community. Show some love today, please. Peace. Have a great day. Respect, respect, respect, and more respect. It saves lives...

Good evening Wishful thinking Wednesday. Yes, we all have times when we are wishing for this or that. Want this to happen or this thought to come true. Most times when you work hard at what you want you often get it and then there are times when it just wasn't time for you. This doesn't mean giving up you just have to work a little harder. Ask God to give you that extra strength to keep pushing on. Don't walk away from your dreams. Much love and have a great night Peace.

Good evening on this beautiful Thursday. We started this week with my name got a meaning, then take control, next was Wishful thinking, I just want to raise your thought process about self. Once we all work on ourselves, there is not much time for anything else. We are forever growing and evolving. Continue to challenge yourself to higher heights. Just because you want more out of life doesn't make you greedy. I'm always thirsty or hungry for knowledge and understanding. May God continue to bless you and have a peaceful night. Peace.

Good evening, Freedom isn't Free Friday. In today's society freedom is not free. We have a price tag on our value today that wasn't in place years ago. We once could drink our tap water today we must buy God-given free spring water. We once could come out at night without fear of being hurt or attacked, now we rather stay home. We once could discipline our children now these courts want to control us all. Freedom isn't Free. We have to pay a price one way or another. What's your freedom Mine is loving my creator and you. Have a blessed night Peace.

Good afternoon, Sisters Saturday. To my beautiful Black Queens. I realize you have been in a war that seems to never end. I hear your plea for help in this world of loneliness, when it seems like no one speaks your language I offer you my ear, I only want to say to you after all these years of pain I'm sorry, I believe in you, I respect you, and God knows I love you. So, Queens please don't give up on us we fighting back strong. From you, all hope survives. May God continue to keep you as I get strong enough to hold you. Peace.

Chapter 8

August

August the hottest month ever.

ANGELS = GOD SENDS HIS ANGELS TO PROTECT US.

URGES = GOD IS CONSTANTLY

SENDING YOU SOMETHING

THAT WILL URGE YOU TO

FOLLOW HIM.

GOD = GOD IS GOOD ALL THE TIME.

USEFUL = THIS WILL BE EXTREMELY USEFUL.

SPIRITUALITY = YOUR SPIRITUALITY IS YOUS
AND YOURS ALONE.

TRUST = TRUST IN GOD AND YOU WON'T
GOWRONG.

GM Save me Sunday. I asked a friend if I was in trouble would you save me, (that friend replied) it all depends on what it is. Now today that's still my friend. I never asked that friend for help because every time I got in trouble. I called on God. I said God please get me out of the situation. God never let me down nor did my friend. See when I needed help God sent her to help me. Having everything I needed. God will always save you just have to recognize the help he sent. So go to God for the help you need and he will send the answer. Dear God, I thank you and my friend for always being there for me. Turning to God saved me he will save you too. Peace love .

Good evening, Mercy Monday. God forever have mercy on me for I am driving to be the best I can be. Have a blessed night Peace.

Good evening Take a Bow Tuesday. Yes, stand up and take a bow you get the best performance act award. You put on quite a show. Now that that's over let's stop acting and be yourself. You have put on your last show it's time to be the King's/Queens, God's/Goddess, Mother's/Father's God wants us to be. Our grandparents and great-grandparents are very upset at how we allowed their villages to fall apart. Dear God bless the reader of this message that he/she will be ready to serve you, God. AMEN, AMEN, AMEN. Have a great and blessed night Peace love.

Good evening (It's My Time) Thursday. Yes, it's your time to shine. Life has its ups/downs, twists/turns, stormy weather, and then there is BRIGHT SUN SHINY DAYS. WE ARE WINNERS so we don't, won't, and can't stay down long. Be proud of who you are because you are beautiful. It's your time to shine. Have a great evening Peace.

Goodnight, Friday Frustrations. Frustrations cloud your judgment and thought process. It's an evil that waits for a weakened moment in your life and attacks. You truly don't know whom or what you are frustrated with. So, look in the mirror it's you. Yes, it's you because you allowed
 the evil in your heart and mind. Now as you calm down you want to know what happened. Dear God protect me from me because I can be my own worse, enemy at times. AMEN, AMEN, AMEN peace.

Good evening, Salute somebody Saturday. My first SALUTE goes out to God. He has truly been all of our rock and strength in the dark hours. Secondly, I SALUTE the beautiful

Queens of the world for you have given blood, sweat, and tears to our people. Without you being a man- heaven it would be far more chaos. Last but not least you are the KINGS of our nation of people. For being the brave hardworking protector and providers of your villages. Know that every day, I thank God for the presence of you both kings/queens. Children you are never forgotten for you, the legacy of our heritage is kept alive. I respect you for honoring your fathers and mothers of earth. Peace. Who loves you (I do) who got you (God do) Know that.

Good afternoon Sharing love Sunday. God shares his love with you every day. He wakes you up and gets you started on your way. He sends you blessings daily. So, in respect for
God's love, I challenge you all to show love today. Tell someone you love them,

give a hug, say thank you to show appreciation for all your blessings. Have a great day Peace.

Good evening on this great day. Manly Monday. Today is to the Men that are manning up and holding it down the best they can with what they got. Once you learn that life isn't about how big your pockets are, or how fancy your car or clothes are you have graduated to a level of manhood many don't get to experience. Your character, your spirit, and your ability to touch people with your kindness are worth much more. Just ask someone and see what they tell you. I thank God for the Men that have risen above their minute egos.

Continue to strive brothers and live life. Much respect and Peace. People let the men in your world know that they are important to you sometimes have a great night.

Good night Thankful Tuesday. Let us pray. Dear God, we come to you in thanks for this day, days before, and days to come. We thank you for the blessings that have come to our doorsteps. We thank you for your watchful angel that keeps us safe from harm. God as we rest this night allow us to rest peacefully and wake with a loving heart. AMEN, AMEN, AMEN. All be safe and happy Peace.

Goodnight, Workshop Wednesday. I pray that your workshop was very productive today. Knowing that you carried God with you in all that you had to do things went well. As you close in for the night say your prayers thanking God for such a peaceful and blessed day. When you wake to Trusting Thursday be ever grateful for the new day Peace and good night.

Gm Trusting Thursday. I've heard there is two things you get every day that God allows you to wake up and that is (A CHANCE AND A CHOICE). Now what you do with your chance is your choice. Make your chance worth the choices you make. Have a great day Peace love you.

Good evening, Family Friday. Dear God, we ask that you continue to bless and watch over our families, friends, and loved ones. I thank you for the years you have given us. AMEN, AMEN. Forever check on your family they need to know you care. Have a great night Peace.

Goodnight Striving to be somebody Saturday. Every day we are awakened by our great God and then we strive to make this day great. Had it not been for his grace and mercy surely, we would have nothing to look forward to. As you strive remember to thank God for that strength and willpower to succeed. Have a blessed and peaceful night Peace love.

Goodnight Saving Sunday. Dear God we all need saving. We come to you asking for forgiveness and your mercy. Amen. Saving starts with you first accepting your creator as the higher power and then asking for his grace. Have a great night Peace love

Good evening Making a difference Monday. Every day we grow to make difference in every life we touch. A difference for all the good that we have inside of us. God, we thank you for molding us in your image and likeness that we will continue to be better people. Know that as we leave a footprint in this world, that it is like yours because today we follow you. AMEN, AMEN, AMEN. Continue to make a difference and do it with love and Peace. Peace have a great night.

Good evening Terrific Tuesday. No matter what you are going through make your day terrific. Be forever encouraged because you will make it through. Doors may close in your face, people may turn their backs on you, you may fall on hard times just know God will carry you through it all.
PEACE and have a great night.

Goodnight Whispering Wednesday. It is known that a loud voice is the voice of a reckless person. A soft-spoken person is a person of great works and words. So, to the people listening for the thunder, it is just noise, the destruction is in the lightning. A Silent flash of light. Be humble my friends and family we see you. Have a great night and Peace. Shhh quiet God is working on you. Love you

Good evening on this Take your Time Thursday. We are in such a hurry that we don't even get to enjoy anything. I want to take my time and experience the joy of this life. This life only happens once the next one might not be so good. Slow down enjoy God's blessings. Dear God, I want to thank you for this life, this chance, and choice every day. AMEN, AMEN, AMEN. Rest peaceful tonight Peace love you.

Good night For Filling Friday. Being fulfilled is a wonderful feeling when you know what it is you are being fulfilled for. Doing the work for God gives me the fulfillment I need. Try it to see how you feel. Have a great night Peace.

Storytelling Saturday. Telling a story can be healthy for some. They can get the toxin out of your mind. Our mind holds many different concepts of life. We are different understand it. PEACE.

Good night Special Sunday. Know that you are special. You were chosen by God to make it here and share your love with his other followers. Always know your worth, have a great night Peace love.

Goodnight, Manic depression Monday. Bringing your attention to things we overlook or just pay no attention to until it affects us directly. Manic depression is known today as bipolar disorder. There are many forms of depression this is just one. Depression leads to suicide. This disease may harm others before it harms the person that has it. Check on your loved ones we can never know what they are going through. I'm here if anyone wants to talk. Dear God watch over us as we sleep and awaken

us with joy and love in our hearts.
AMEN, AMEN, AMEN. Have a great night
Peace.
Goodnight, thank you, Tuesday. Let us
give thanks to God for waking us this
morning, for watching over us through
the day and as we prepare to rest for the
night, we thank his angels for watching
us as we sleep. AMEN, AMEN, AMEN. I
want to give a special thanks to you yes
you for loving me. PEACE, and love you
also.

Goodnight Where do I stand Wednesday.
There is no doubt in it I stand with you
God. You allow me to rise in the morning
and grant me a peaceful night. I once
didn't know what FAITH and LOYALTY
were until I took a look at my life and see
what you are doing for me. The strongest
need someone to lean on and you have
been my rock and post to lean on. Your
work on me has restored my faith that

there are good men/women in this cruel world. Everyone, with God, is where you should stand, and rest assured your life will come together. AMEN, AMEN, AMEN. Have a blessed and safe night Peace.

Good evening, Teaching Thursday. Teaching Thursday is dedicated to the mothers of today. I want to thank you for your strength, your dedication to being the best mother you can be. You are our futures first teacher. It is through you that this world is formed. Dear God bless these mothers, keep them safe and unharmed. AMEN, AMEN, AMEN. The woman is a born nurturing spirit. Have a great night as we salute you Peace. Love you, beautiful Queens.

Good evening, Feelings Friday. Feelings often overlooked by others, hurt by many, needed for most, yet personally, we all claim we don't have them. Lol.

Untrue, we all have feelings some just go deeper than others. So today we learn to respect everyone's feelings. Have a great feeling night Peace love you.

Good night Staying Strong Saturday. Together we are strong. Staying together we are unbreakable. Have a great night Peace love you.

Good evening, Survivor Sunday. Surviving all life's ups and downs is our testimony for today. We are winners of life's dramas. I believe in you all, you have weathered all storms and we owe it all to the grace of God. Through God is where all things are possible. Dear God, we come to you and thank you for your protection and saving. AMEN, AMEN, AMEN. Have a great night Peace.

Good evening Making life count Monday. Family and friends today we are MAKING

LIFE COUNT. The things you do from this point on make it worth something and make it mean and represent something. The people around you make them mean something and show them that they do. No more NEGATIVITY IN YOUR LIFE. Dear God thank you for clearing my life of negativity and blessing me with a heart of truth. AMEN, AMEN, AMEN. Have a great start at making your life count. Peace.

Good evening, Taste of Class Tuesday. Men/women in all that you do have a taste of class with it. We can get so messy and caught up in the showing-off part that you become tasteless. You can turn something beautiful into something ugly. My Strong Black King's/Queens I know you are unique so show it gracefully. Have a great evening Peace, and a great night Peace.

Chapter 9

September

SURVIVOR = GOD CREATED SURVIVORS.

ETERNITY = ETERNITY LIVES WITH THE

CREATOR AND THE CREATOR ALONE.

POWER = GOD GAVE YOU A SOURCE OF POWER LIKE NO OTHER.

TEMPTATION = TEMPTATION ALL AROUND YOU EVERYDAY AND NIGHT

EMPOWERED = EMPOWERED WITH A STRENGTH GIVEN BY GOD

MEMBERS = WE ARE MEMBERS OF A DIVINE

UNIVERSE. BUILDING = BUILDING BRIDGES AND NOT

TEARING THEM DOWN.

ENJOYING = LIFE IS WORTH ENJOYING.

RIGHTEOUSNESS = WE TRY TO BE AS RIGHTEOUS AS POSSIBLE

Good night Won't, God, Make a WAY Wednesday. Yes, when you put things to prayer and work hard at it. God will make a way for success. We have put enough in man's hands now put it in God's hands. Are you tired of never getting it right, well stop leaving God out Dear God we trust in you, we are ready to allow you control My faith is strong and my path is clear show us your way AMEN, AMEN, AMEN Have a great night Peace.

Goodnight Turning back Time Thursday. I want to turn back the time for some very valuable lessons. See our grandparent parents taught some very important things that was passed down to the next generation. Somewhere the passing down stopped or the children stopped listening and taking heed to what was given to them. We need to share some of those lost lessons. I remember when my parents and grandparents would give a look and the block went quiet. I remember when I love you really meant I love you. What do you remember? Have a blessed night Peace.

Good evening Focusing Friday. There is nothing like a man/woman that is totally focused. Their drive is intoxicating it will take you on a high like no other. The only thing higher is the drive you have when you are focused and you got God first with all you do. A focused mind with God you're stronger than you know. Dear God keep us focused and blessed. AMEN, AMEN, AMEN. Have a blessed night Peace love you.

Goodnight, Starving Saturday. Dear God our souls, spirit, bodies, and minds are STARVING for your glorious food. God feeds us the language of love peace and harmony. Lift us up and carry us to your kingdom. AMEN, AMEN, AMEN. As we sit in hunger know that the meal we need is coming. Have a blessed night Peace.

Good evening Speechless Sunday. It is time for you to speak up yet you are speechless. It is time for you to add your 2cents again you are speechless. It's time for you to speak on what you believe and you are silent. Why is it when the time comes and opportunity is knocking, we get tongue tired or lost for words? You should go on a silent fast so when you do speak something worthwhile will come out your mouth. Dear God give me the words to say and when I should say them. Equip me with the language my people love and understand. AMEN, AMEN, AMEN. Have a quiet night Peace.

Good night Moving Monday. Standing still gets you nowhere. We are moving, moving forward, and achieving what we set out to get. Prayer works as you MOVE toward what you are praying for. Stop sitting and move something. Dear God keep us moving forward. AMEN, AMEN, AMEN. Have a great night Peace love you.

Goodnight Take my hand Tuesday. Allow God to take your hand and guide you to better things. We grab hold of things not fully understanding them. If it was that easy for you to hold a man/woman hand and follow allow God to take your hand should be a piece of cake. Reach out for God. have a great night Peace.

Good afternoon Will you Wednesday. Will you continue to strive for greatness, will you learn to stay calm in unknown territory, will you love before dislike, and most of all WILL YOU get to know God. There can be a lot of will you just know that I believe you can. Have a great rest of your day Peace.

Goodnight Tug a war Thursday. (Tug- a-war) yes, there is a force that's pulling and pushing at your inner being. Men and women are strangely mixed with a Higher self and a Lower self. These two forces are constantly in a battle to see who will control that person. At some point in time, we all have fallen victim to our lower self to whom we should learn from our mistakes of yesterdays. Now we know that the Higher self-controls the greater part of our life. The higher self is the God inside you. Stay in your higher self it is more rewarding. Peace love you.

Good night Frantic Friday. Lots of times we run around in a frantic trying to figure things out. Never enough time, things just not falling into place, feeling overwhelmed, emotions running on overload. When this happens be still pause yourself and pray. Give all these things to God and he will help you work it out. We are a people that refuse to say (I need help) but at times we do. Stop being so pride struck and take it to God if you can't ask anyone to help. Have a great night. And in the voice of a great friend (God got you) Peace.

Goodnight, Superman Saturday. Yes, this is for the Men that step up to the plate Every time he is needed and gets the job done. We stand strong in the midst of all the odds. Men Continue to prevail and grow mentally, emotionally, and most of all spiritually. You are great

Peace. Ladies give these great men and applause. Thanks

Good morning Setting the record Straight Sunday. My upbringing was profound. Involved parents raised me right. Things went wrong when I wanted to take several classes at different schools of learning. I took a class on Jxxx Axx one on one at a night class at Stupid Stay university. Graduated from there and desired to get a Doctrine degree in Braindead community college at Don't give a Fxxx academy. I didn't think that was enough so went for my masters at Crash Dummy Reformatory. As I walked around noticing people staying away from me, I just couldn't understand. I thought I had everything a well-respected man should have. I came across this building with its doors open so I walked in. This was the turning point in my life. A man and woman greeted me with a warm greeting and handed me a booklet. Inside I found a map. Its title was (Your road to success). This pamphlet had a total of three pages. The first page was " FIND GOD " second " KNOW WHO YOU ARE " last page " MOVE FORWARD". Finding God, understanding who I am, and always moving forward changed my life. I realized I didn't know anything until I learned about these three things. Have a blessed Sunday Peace.

Goodnight, Monday Madness. The madness of maneuvering around society these days has gotten to be so crazy. How did we get to the point when human contact can be fatal Children can't freely play with other kids without parents being in fear of what is known as COVID-19. The talk about the poor middle class and upper class is no more. We only hear about killings and COVID-19. So, I say love who is loving you and love them hard because tomorrow only brings death and disease. I love you Peace. God bless us all.

Goodnight Making it happen Monday. Yes, God makes it happen for us to get things done every day. So, we thank him for all he does. Now, what are you going to do? Make it happen, you are a true winner when you put your heart and mind to it. Know God and I believe in you. Have a blessed night Peace.

Gm Workshop Wednesday. Know that there is a workshop for all parts of your life and you must maintain an active responsibility of working on it. We get lazy, thrown off track, and sometimes just don't give a ___. To get what you desire you must put in that work. I work hard at what I want physically, mentally, and emotionally. You do the same. Have a great day and Peace.

Good night THINKING THURSDAY. Knowing that thought is the cause of all things that come to exist, we must do much better with our thought process. We waste time thinking about things we can't control and no time on the things we can. Our thoughts are powerful recognize them. Dear God put some greater thoughts on our minds. AMEN, AMEN, AMEN. Have a great night Peace love you.

Goodnight Following directions Friday. Direction who's to say we are moving in the right direction... Forward you still may stumble. Backward could be avoiding a major problem. Side to side sometimes you must change lanes to stay on course. Down could be just easing the load and not going rock bottom. Circles, well sometimes we have to revisit some things to move on past them and fully understand. All these directions just help you grow into a wholesome MAN or WOMAN.

So, look at your direction now as a constant improvement, not a set- back.

Also, learn to use your roadside assistance to help you navigate through life. Stay up, people. Much love from the have a great night Peace love ….

Goodnight, Structure Saturday. Needing structure is something we all need. Its rules apply to all parts of living. Religious structure, economical structure, financial structure etc. Everything has its structure and laws once violated things are out of control. Embrace structure it will keep you focused. As you put things in order keep your structure. Have a great night Peace love you.

Goodnight, Starving Sunday. A starving man/woman always makes a way to eat. The question is what are you starving for. Do you know what you are hungry for or what will it take to fill you up As I take a glance at the world we are starving for a spiritual and soulful meal? The meal that only comes from God. God has prepared a feast as it is written in all books of understanding for the souls and hearts of men/women. Will you be eating at that table or do you want to continue to eat at the table of the wicked Feed your hunger, feed it the food it needs. Learn how to eat to live and not live to eat. Have a blessed night Peace.

Good evening Mighty Monday. What is mightier than the tongue? A tongue with an intelligent brain and something to say. What is mightier than a group of black men and women?

A group of STRONG BLACK MEN AND WOMEN WITH AN EDUCATED PURPOSE. What is mightier than a large family? A village of families that has God and love uniting them as one family. With God and prayer, all these mighty things are in your reach. Have a mighty night Peace love you.

Good evening Thank you, Tuesday. I just want to say thank you to God and to you. Know that your presence in my life is noticed. Thank you and have a great rest of your day. Peace and love.

Working it out Wednesday. I know I'm late lol. As we look at the issues that are ruining our city, we only blame our youth. Yes, they are in fact out of control, but some of God's wildest creatures are controlled through love. Our youth are missing love. Also, the lack of guidance. There are many other issues that are destroying our city we just don't see them because all they are showing is black kids killing black kids. Just something to think about, how do we begin to save them. Peace!

Good night Together Thursday. Let's get it all TOGETHER. We are so divided as a people and family. I give a big applause to the ones that got it together. I solute, the families that conduct themselves as one unit. For those that got it together stand up and help get the rest of our people together. Sleep on that and have a blessed night Peace.

Goodnight, Forgiveness Friday. Men and women engage themselves into different things in life. All these things come with consequences. We ask for forgiveness even when we know we just might do this again. That's the beauty in knowing God, he will forgive us Every time, we ask for forgiveness. When do we stop asking for forgiveness and just do the right thing Have a great night Peace love you.

Goodnight (Stop) Saturday. Stop what you are doing and give a giant thank you to God for this beautiful day. (STOP) What you are doing and give that one or two you can count on a hug and thank them for always being there. (STOP) and look in that mirror and thank yourself for never giving up. It's the moment that you need to just stop what you are doing and take a deep breath and sometimes you just want to let out a good cry. These are the times when you just have to STOP. Have a blessed night Peace.

Goodnight Softer side Sunday. (Listen to me for a second)" Lil man dont cry toughen up- go hard my nxxxx, you can't care about anything in these streets. " Many of us was told these words and many of us have shared these words with some Lil child. Sad isn't it that now we want to see the softer side of our youth but we only taught them how to be stoic to everything. Momma would say be very careful of what you wish for it will bite you right on your butt. Well as we ask now that our youth stop with the madness, we need to watch what we teach them early on in life. Just something to think about have a great night Peace.

Good evening, Momma Monday. Thanks to you all day, every day, mothers that put in that needed time with your children regardless of what life has put in your way. You are the super she-roes of this day and time. We are thankful for your love and support. Your care hasn't gone unnoticed. You all have a great night. Dear God bless these strong mothers for all that they do. Peace.

Ps. to all you females that are acting as parents you are seen also. Thank you as well.

Good night Tell your Story Tuesday. Everyone has a story to tell. Some stories are fascinating, some dramatic, some tragic, some made from a fairytale, nevertheless your story is your story. It made you the man/woman you are today. Learn to embrace your story and get from it all the lessons God sent to you.

We all have work to do on self but be ever so proud of the work we have done. Hold your head up for you are a winner no matter your story. Have a great night Peace Love U!

Goodnight, Wisdom Wednesday. Wisdom is acquired over time. Years of making mistakes and starting over again. Wisdom is proof that you followed the footprints in the sand that God left for you to follow. Wisdom is that stage of life where you appreciate all your life journeys. Congratulations to you, you have passed many- tests. Have a great night Peace.

Goodnight, Tip the scale Thursday. At times you find the strength and energy to tip the scale. This is gaining the edge on your dreams. Tipping the scale means stepping up higher than most, overleaping the boundaries that tie you to limiting yourself to not pushing harder. We tip the scale because we are winners and we dream big. Continue to rip the scale never settle for less than what God has given you. Have a great night Peace.

Chapter 10

October

OBEDIENCE = OBEDIENCE TO GOD IS NEEDED IN THE WORLD TODAY.

CONTROL = SELF-CONTROL SOMETHING WE LACK.

TRAINING = TRAINING AND STUDY OF SELF.

OUTCOME = THE OUTCOME OF STUDYING IS ACHIEVEMENT.

BATTLE = THERE IS A BATTLE TO BECOME SUCCESSFUL.

EAGER = NEVER LOSE YOUR EAGERNESS TO BE GREAT.

REMEMBER = REMEMBER THE ROUGHNESS OF YOUR CLIMB TO GREATNESS.

Goodnight, Father Friday. I want to say to the fathers of this day and time thank you. Thank you for your dedication to being a great father. Often times fathers get a bad rep because it's been proven that we often walk off. So, men continue to stand strong and raise their children. Father's you are appreciated and needed. Again, thanks for being a real FATHER. Have a great night Peace.

Goodnight Somebody loves you Saturday. Sometimes we need to know this very important thing. Dear God let us thank you for your forever-giving love. You all have a blessed night knowing you are loved. God loves you and so do I. Peace love U!

Goodnight, Sound off Sunday. Ok, it's sound off Sunday so let's start off with giving a holla for God and all His blessings. Second, we going to give a holla for your focus on your goals and dreams. Next, we just going to give a shout to the ones that have believed in you from the start. Thank you all. Peace. HOLLA

Goodnight, Mask Monday. Everyone is so tired of wearing these, mask yet we have been wearing masks for years. Masks that if removed will people understand you yet like you. We all have to put on our masks just to deal with society. So, masks are here to stay. Mask Monday, yes you can yell now. I do. Have a great night Peace love you.

Goodnight, Takeover Tuesday. The take-over is real. God has come to take control of his people. Dear God we the children of you (most high) return to your way. We as MEN stand strong taking care of our families providing for them, and before you stand our WOMEN raising and teaching our little ones the ways of God. We thank you for always providing what we need. As we rest for the night send your angels to keep us safe. AMEN, AMEN, AMEN peace love U.

Goodnight Who am I Wednesday. (Who are you?) Even the people we have known for years sometimes ask you that question. When asked that question, we get so offended but why. When we are forever changing it is easy not to be recognized. A person that is constantly working on themselves will get that question. Don't stop working on yourself and changing for the better. Have a great night Peace.

Goodnight Thankful Thursday. Many of us don't really know the rough side of living. Don't know what it means to want for a little relief. Life has us in a chokehold and we are pleading for air. Some say they know the struggle yet they won't even take the time to thank God for all the times that air has been provided to you, that relief came when you were ready to give up. You never had to dig deep down inside of yourself to face the next day. God saw you through it all. He held your hand walking with you along your difficult journey. So, tonight we give THANKS TO THE GREAT CREATOR FOR ALL HE HAS DONE. THANK YOU, GOD, AMEN, AMEN, AMEN. PEACE.

Goodnight Highly Favored Friday. You are highly favored and forever blessed. So, I have a question. (Do you know your worth?) Knowing your worth allows you to see just why you are highly favored and forever blessed. Repeat. I have no monetary value my worth exceeds any and all amounts of money. My God created me in his image and likeness so my value is unpriceable. Have a great night. Peace love you

Goodnight Studying Saturday. What do you study? (Self) and (all things about God). The study of self is because we are forever changing. I study things about God because we are created in his image and likeness. Continue to study it is your greatest path to happiness. You may find some sad things along the way but in the end, there is pure happiness. Have a great night Peace love you.

Goodnight Sweet Sunday. As we end our weekend and move forward to our work week go into it with joy. It's a blessing from one day to the next. I thank you, God for blessing me. I thank you for continuously waking us up to receive your gift of life.
Thank you AMEN, AMEN, AMEN. Have a blessed night Peace.

Goodnight, Mic check Monday. 1, 2 mic check I need you to say thank you to God for his Deliverance of each and every day. I want you to say just how blessed you are. Have a wonderful night Peace love you.

Goodnight, Thoughtfulness Tuesday. How many of you can honestly say that you are thoughtful to the next person's feelings Not many because we are taught that our own feelings are more important than anyone else's. Which is okay until you just totally disregard theirs altogether. Don't be so thoughtless to others. Have a thoughtful night Peace love you.

Goodnight, Wednesday. Dear God continue to give us the strength to stand the tests of time, and the wisdom to see your wonderful blessings. AMEN, AMEN, AMEN. Sometimes are made to test your faith, belief, and trust in God. Be strong and overcome your fears. Have a blessed and peaceful night Peace.

Goodnight Thankful Thursday. It's a great feeling to be loved. Dear God thank you for your love and mercy. Thank you for putting the right people in my life. AMEN, AMEN, AMEN. Love can hurt but it is also wonderful when you are truly loved. Have a great night Peace.

Goodnight, Fortune Friday. Do you know what your fortunes are?

(NO) because your fortunes come in the form of $'s and cents.

So, you miss your own value just as you miss your fortunes. I tell you often to know your value and now recognize your fortune. Your first fortune is, (you are covered by a mighty God that wakes you every day). Next, (you have a roof over your head, food to eat). The small things that you call (perks) of life are fortunes. Everyone doesn't have them. Have a great night Peace love you.

Goodnight, Saturday. Prayer, prayer, prayer. We all need prayer. Have a great night. Peace love you.

Good evening Special Sunday. Dear God thank you for another special Sunday. Thank you for your forgiveness and thank you for sending your angels out to watch over us every day. AMEN, AMEN, AMEN. Continue to be forever thankful. Have a wonderful evening. Peace love you!

Goodnight Meaningful Monday. As our lives move in whatever direction, we need to be very attentive so that we can absorb all the lessons. Some directions take our attention off the lessons that we are to learn. As it is said for every action there is a reaction. Be more attentive to your life people. Dear God as you watch over us as we sleep cover us with good kind thoughts, rid our hearts of any hatred and ill feelings. We need peace. AMEN, AMEN, AMEN. Have a great night Peace, love you.

Goodnight Trustful Tuesday. In God we trust, is written on money. Is this why we want so much of it? Written in our religious books it says to trust in the Lord God. Yet I don't hear us needing more of this. We need to trust in the Lord God, not the money that says in God we trust. have a great night Peace, love you

Goodnight Working together Wednesday. Today is about working together. As it is known to most " together we stand divided we fall". Where did our people become so divided, We, are full of self-destruction, self-hate, to the point where we project it onto others. The news gives you images of pain and unloved people.

We need to get back to being a unit of love and togetherness. God has watched over us, now we need to watch over each other. Have a marvelous night Peace, love you.

Good evening, Talk about it Thursday. Talk about it because keeping it bottled up inside you will hurt more in the long run. Keeping things closed up inside is a leading factor of stress, headaches, suicide, and more. Having someone to talk to is very meaningful. If you don't have someone please talk to God. Our society is plagued with different illnesses today, we need help. Hey you I'm here if you want to talk. Have a great night Peace love you.

Goodnight, Family, and Friends Friday. You got family that treats you like a friend and friends that treat you like family. When family treats you like a friend they will cross you, when your friend treats you like family, they are loyal to you for life. Choose your friends wisely and watch your family closely. Have a great night Peace, love you

Goodnight Stop the madness Saturday. As a collective whole, we have to figure out how to stop the madness that is troubling our world. For one we have to start with finding God. With God in our life, we can't go wrong. Next, we must start loving each other, encouraging one another, and protecting our children and women. There once was a time where we felt safe in our neighborhood. Now we are living in fear of sitting on the porch after dark. Children are so disrespectful for lack of love and strong guidance. Let us get it together. Say your prayers and have a blessed night Peace, love you.

Goodnight, Superwoman Sunday. You beautiful Queens get up each day blocking out the pain and disappointment of the world. You hold your head up high and you do what a real woman should do. Push forward and be that teacher, nurturer, and mother. I will be the first to say thank you for always being strong when we as men fall short. I will say that we are trying to do better. Thanks again and know that God is forever watching over you. Have a blessed night Peace love you.

Goodnight, Manpower Monday. Men listen up, listen closely it is time we step our performance up to a level that is above the level we have been given. Men don't do the bare minimum we do more. Men don't want to be asked we are doing the thing before that. Men are protectors and providers. We don't have time for (I can't nor let me see) we are men that get the job done. Men, I salute you for standing strong never quitting. Have a great night great Men. Peace, love you.

Goodnight, Time to love Tuesday. In this day and time, we need to love on those that love us. Many different things are happening today that for some tomorrow never comes. So, I don't and won't wait to show my love. If it's real then there shouldn't be a problem showing it. Everyone needs to know they are loved so tell them that you do. I want you to know you are appreciated and loved. Have a blessed night Peace, love you!

Goodnight, Workshop Wednesday. Back in the work/shop. No, our work on ourselves is never done. As life moves us forward things change so we grow and adapt to all situations. Changing and growing are two characteristics that give defining measures to who you are as a person. Continue to grow and accept the change. As always when things get tough pray and pray some more. It will work its way out. Taken from the playbook of a great friend (GOD GOT YOU). HAVE A BEAUTIFUL NIGHT. Peace, love you!

Goodnight Thinking Thursday. The thought is the cause of it all.
Through thinking, we create our destiny. Think before you act has been a saying that has been true through time. As we sit and think of the things that God has blessed of with, think of how do we ever repay Him for his acts of continuous blessings. Have a great thought-provoking night Peace love you.

Goodnight, Freedom Friday. What is freedom when you are still held captive by your own fears? Success is for those that rise above their fear of failure. Accomplishments are for those that step up to the challenge. Break the chain that controls you. Free yourself of your own mental struggles. Have a blessed night Peace, love you!

Goodnight Somebody loves you Saturday. Yes, without doubt, nor contradiction God loves you. He has loved you from day one. He has continued to bless you and care for you even when you don't love yourself. So, we stand here and give a special shoutout to God for being our rock. As an added bonus God allowed me to love you as well. Have a wonderful night Peace love you.

Goodnight Saving souls one at a time Sunday. Hey, I know a place that will say your soul. It's over on Forgiveness Blvd. Once on forgiveness Blvd, there is this building you can go into named Redemption Hall. The professor there likes to talk about self-building. He often sends you out on field trips with other professors of different schools of thought to help you find your way. I think it's wise that we all take this journey to these nearby lands. You will be very surprised at what you find. So, as you take your journey into saving your soul keep an open mind because God will reveal to you lots of things. Have a blessed night Peace love you.

Chapter 11

November

NOVEMBER IS THE MONTH OF GIVING THANKS.

NATION = TOGETHER WE ARE A STRONG NATION.

OBEDIENCE = BE OBEDIENT TO GOD.

VICTORIOUS = VICTORY COMES WHEN YOU SEE IT THROUGH

EVERLASTING = OUR SOUL AND SPIRIT WILL HAVE EVERLASTING LIFE.

MORAL = YOUR MORALS SHOULD BE HIGHER THAN YOUR WANTS.

BRAVERY =DON'T CONFUSE BRAVERY WITH STUPIDITY

EDUCATION = EDUCATION IS A MUST-HAVE.

RUINS = WE OFTEN RUIN OUR OWN LIVES.

Goodnight My time Monday. Today is about you. Look in the mirror and tell yourself it's okay to have time for just you. Often times we need to decompress. It is nothing wrong with it either. So, don't feel bad because you made today about only you. Give yourself a hug, and kiss, a pat on the back etc. You have been the rock for everyone else and now it is your time. God continues to bless you in all that you do. Have a great night Peace, love you.

Goodnight, Tuesday. Time and time again we are given a chance to get things right. First, you must know where you went wrong. At one point in life, we believed that we could do it all on our own. We gave credit to the man for our success in life and we blamed God for all the bad and wrong in our life asking (God why have forsaken me) when in fact it we you that had forsaken God. God has and is the one and only constant in your life. Everyone else is a gift from God. Dear

God in our weakness please forgive us, as you have done time and time again. Amen. As you rest tonight, I pray you awake with a new beginning and a heart of love. Have a blessed night Peace, love you

Good evening, Where have you been Wednesday? Well, beings though I am created in the image and likeness of God just for a moment I want to ask some questions that God want answers to. God wants to know where were you when he got the sun to rise to brighten your day but you slept all day. Where were you when he sent the messenger looking for you to answer your prayer, where were you when your people (family) needed a warrior to protect them. Where were you when that child needed a father/mother? Where were you?????? Yet you get on your knees and say God where are you when I need you most. God has and will always be there it's your turn to show up.

Let everyone stand up and be counted for. Dear God, I am here present and counted for. Where are you? Have a great night Peace, love you.

Goodnight, Thoughtfulness Thursday. Being thoughtful is very good. We all must do our part in being thoughtful to others. Have a blessed night Peace, love you

Goodnight Fabulous Friday. In life, one should always know that they are fabulous. You are fabulous in the way you serve God, in the way you carry yourself, in the way you communicate, in the way you listen. Your character speaks volumes of who you are. I want you to also know I'm proud of you. Have a blessed and wonderful night Peace, love you.

Goodnight STOP. Saturday. Stop what you doing and give God a thank you for getting you to this day. Stop and thank God for never giving up on you. Stop, stop, stop, and thank God for the Grace and Mercy. Now stop with your neglecting him for all he has done. Remember to thank and honor God each and every day. Have a great night Peace, love you!

Goodnight Spiritual Sunday. In the spirit of peace, love, and unity your spirituality stands out. When these principles are applied to your daily living how can you go wrong? When we allow the true spirit of God to flow through our minds and hearts joy fills the universe. Have a beautiful night Peace, love you

Goodnight, Memories Monday. Do you remember when we use to play outside until the street lights came on Do you remember when our neighborhood was a strong together village, Do, you remember when grandparents were in every household helping raise all the children, Do, you remember when your parents, neighbors, siblings, would give each other hugs of true and real love. Yes, memories of a time that we don't see anymore. So sad where did our love go? With this memory, I want to thank God for not letting me forget it and for allowing me to get that kind of love. In memory of a time that will never be forgotten. Have magical night Peace, love you.

Good evening Take it from me Tuesday. Yes, take it from me prayer works, putting your trust in God works, believing in that force that gives you, life works, better days are coming is true. We have tried many- things, we have given wrong our all for far too long, get your affairs in order, it's time to live right, be right with God. I believe in you. You have been made KINGS AND QUEENS now let's go get God's people in order. Have a magnificent night Peace, love you.

Goodnight Working on me Wednesday. Working on me for me and God. We develop and change every day so it's a challenge to keep up with ourselves so we shouldn't have time to chase whatever somebody else got going on. We grow in all areas of life. Have a great time growing goodnight. Peace, love you!

Goodnight Talk to me Thursday. Let's talk, we have put men/women on this spiritual pedestal for their God-like ways and actions. Are you not like these men/women, don't you have the ability to conduct yourself just as they do? You want the benefits of being connected to God but you don't want to do the works. God has prepared you to continue his work here on earth. Let's band together to make our paradise on earth also. Much respect and love to you have a blessed night Peace, love you!

Goodnight, Freeway Friday. Traveling down a lonely highway. A highway of righteousness. I'm headed for greatness and anyone with this mindset is free to come along. We will be changing our ways, cleaning up our acts, forgiving ourselves as well as others, we will be dedicating our actions to God, and loving not hating. All aboard this ride are heading out for greatness. Have a great night Peace, love you!!

Goodnight, Saturday. What do you see when you look in the mirror? Can you see your likeness to God? Can you feel the presence of God guiding you in your walk today? Yes, question after question to make you think. We are critical of ourselves so if we will be then be critical to make you a better person. Have a blessed night Peace, love you!

Good evening, Sad but true Sunday. Life gives and life takes. The universe operates like a boomerang, what you throw out there is sure to return one day. You pray to God, he answers. You do God's work he rewards you. Anything other than that is uncivilized. So, since we are creatures that love rewards, our ways should change drastically. We need to be putting love and peace out into the universe. Have a blessed night Peace, love you.

Goodnight, Monday. Men/women, I'm so proud of you. Your strength is an example of your greatness. Your care is an example of gods, grace. Your spirit is a showing of his existence. Continue to show the world that with God, we will make it. Forever be blessed and show love. Have a great night Peace, love you.

Goodnight (Tis the season to be thankful) Tuesday. Being thankful should be an everyday season. We should not wait for different holidays to express our joy. Having life, love, and Peace is worth celebrating every day. I wake up with a smile and I lay down at night with a smile. You should do the same. You have received more blessings than you can count. Rejoice in the love God has given us constantly. Have a great night Peace, love you.

Goodnight You are a Wonderful Woman Wednesday. You, yes you. I'm talking to you, gods, greatest creation (WOMAN). You are the key and strength that keeps our family unit together. I want to give you a special THANK YOU tonight to let you know your work is very much appreciated and noticed. Each day of your life should be celebrated to show you how much we appreciate you. Your greatness has allowed us to survive. You are loved. Have a great night Peace, love you.

Goodnight, Truth Thursday. My truth for today is (I love me) and you should love yourself as well. It doesn't make you shallow nor does it make you vain. It is times that you must put yourself first. The way you love yourself lets people know you know how to love. So, tonight enjoy loving yourself. Have a good night Peace, love you.

Goodnight Feeling blessed Friday. You should feel blessed each moment God allows you breathe to breath. God has strengthened you with a certain strength that no one can take from you. He gave you a gift and with that gift you are to reach out to others to give them hope and inspiration. Continue with your gift and reach as far out as you can. Have a great night Peace, love you.

Goodnight, Storytime Saturday. Here we are once again with these holiday seasons. Thanksgiving, Christmas, New Year's, kwanza all of which have a story behind them. Well, we as a people have a story to tell also. Tell your children the story of how we loved each other in the past, how we got to know what it was to play outside without fear of being harmed. So, this year instead of talking about Thanksgiving give thanks to God for our past, instead of giving gifts for Christmas give the gift of love. Instead of bringing in a New Year let's start Anew Year. Happy storytelling and cheers to a new beginning. Have a good night Peace, love you.

Good evening Something about your name Sunday. Yes, the song says (there is something about the name Jesus) well I want you to know there is something about your name as well. Your name has value, your name has a purpose. Your given name by your parents. That name represents greatness. So, today you need to step into the role your name represents. That name will be spoken even when your time has come to pass. There is something about your name. Have a blessed night Peace, love you.

Goodnight, ME, ME, ME Monday. Yes, tonight is about you and you alone. We all need (ME TIME) these moments allow you many helpful tools. When having your (ME TIME) reflect on all the things that have taken place in your life. The good, (be humble and thankful to God for them), the bad, (understand the lessons that were there for you to learn) then create a positive twist on them. When you can be critical of yourself you are ready for your next phase in life. You are growing into a mature individual. So, enjoy your (ME TIME) you deserve it. Have a great night Peace, love you.

Goodnight, Tuesday. Where do you pick up joy when you are constantly carrying pain and anger? Because you are not accustomed to the reaction of joy and happiness you would rather stay in the norm of pain and confusion. Sadly, our people are so familiar with suffering that the sign of joy scares them. Walk away from your fear of happiness and embrace it. Joy and peace feel so good. Have a great night Peace. Love you!!

Goodnight, Wishing on a star Wednesday. Wishing for better days is a prayer we all should be praying. Continue to pray because prayer works. Have a blessed night Peace, love you.

Good evening, thanks for giving Thursday. I want to thank each of you for giving love. There is nothing more important than showing love to each other. Love is one of life's necessities. We need it. Without it, this world will continue to fall apart. When our children stop loving we should have known we were in trouble. So, again thank you for giving love. Have a blessed night Peace, love you!

Goodnight Forward progress Friday. Forward progress is what we all should be doing. The direction we move determines where we end up in life. Turn on your navigation and type in God and you will be on your way to greatness. When you take your life in the direction of God, you then and only then begin your change.

I'm moving forward towards God anyone want a ride? Have a blessed night Peace, love you.

Goodnight, Super (man/woman) Saturday. Somewhere inside you live a superhero. I can tell you that all day and night but you must believe there is such a person inside you. You have to believe that you can jump over hurdles, stand in a storm, ride the biggest wave. You have to push yourself to the max. God got you so reach for that star. You are a winner. Have a good night Peace, love you.

Goodnight, Spending time, not money Sunday. This is something we need to work on. We often think money can change the emptiness of time. So, this year give your time not your money. Money comes and go but time can't be replaced. Time also carry-on money don't. Spend some time with your children, parents, grandparents, siblings.

Have a great night it doesn't cost you anything. Peace, love you.

Goodnight, too Much to do Monday. There is always too much to do when you are cleaning up your life. If you are dedicating your time and energy to cleaning up your life, you will stay busy. There is always forward progress. Happy cleaning and stay focused. Have a good night Peace, love you.

Goodnight, Thinking thoughts Tuesday. Thinking is easy. We are always in some kind of thought. Acting them out is where the difficulty comes in. Our ideas come to mind like a storm yet unlike a storm we find ourselves standing still. If our actions could be as strong as our thoughts, we all would be working for ourselves. Let us connect our thoughts with our actions see what happens. Have a great night thinking. Peace, love you

Chapter 12

December

December is a joyful month for children and adults looking for gifts for Christmas.

DETERMINATION = DETERMINATION IS ALL ABOUT FOCUS.

EVALUATION = EVALUATE YOURSELF BEFORE YOU EVALUATE SOMEONE ELSE.

COMMUNICATION = COMMUNICATE WITH GOD BEFORE YOU TALK TO ANYONE ELSE.

ECONOMICAL = HAVE SELF ECONOMICAL VALUE.

MANAGEMENT = LEARN TO MANAGE YOURSELF.

BELOVED = YOU ARE BELOVED BY GOD.

EMOTIONAL = BEING LOVED IS VERY EMOTIONAL.

READY = IM READY TO DEDICATE MY LIFE TO GOD.

Good evening, Will you be there Wednesday? The question comes, will you be there when I need you most? Don't ask that question because that person has always been there. They have never let you down you just can't see it through the things you are going through. See me and God has always been there you just didn't see us. God Carry you the distance and I was there to encourage you to continue on. God hired me to let you know change is possible, change is coming, and change is worth the wait. So, yes God will be there in the morning and night and I'll be close by. Enjoy your night Peace, love you.

Goodnight, Tornado Thursday. Yes, God created tornados and other storms to see how and if we can get through them in one piece. Life is the greatest obstacle in the world. It will make and break many. So, every day we go to God and ask that he carry us through all the storms. It is when you think you got it alone that you go spinning out of control. Stay with God and things will be alright. Have a blessed night Peace, love you.

Goodnight, Freeway Friday. I am learning to love to travel and when I'm on the freeway of learning and growing that road trip is absolutely the best. It clears your mind and open it up for God to fill it with great things. Your creative thoughts are ready for growing into something beautiful. God will be picking people up on Redemption Ave headed for Greatness Terr. All you need is an open mind see you there. Have a great night Peace, love you.

Goodnight Standing strong Saturday. Standing you will always be because you understand that you must get back up. Strong is your inheritance from God and no matter what comes your way you make it through. So, STANDING STRONG YOU WILL ALWAYS BE. Have a blessed night Peace, love you

Good evening, Searching for a reason Sunday. If you are searching for a reason we'll let me, tell you that you are the reason. You are the reason to carry on, you are the reason to never give up, you are the reason. God molded you with a special ingredient and the ingredient is above all other toppings you put on. So, when you want to know what the reason is, look in the mirror. If you don't see that special ingredient, call me and I'll tell you. That special ingredient is God, God put a lot of him and a little bit of you in his creating of you. Search no further for that reason know that you are the reason. Have a tremendous night Peace you.

Good morning Making it happen Monday. Today is your day to make it happen. You are the controller of all great things that will happen in your life. Be blessed and be great today.
Have a blessed day Peace love you.

Good morning, all.
Dear GOD, I COME TO YOU BROKEN AND LOST FOR I DON'T KNOW MY WAY. (THIS IS THE CRY WE ALL HAVE SPOKEN

AT SOME POINT) FOR WE KNOW THAT THE HEALING WE SEEK ONLY COMES FROM GOD AND GOD ALONE. SO, I (Michael) SAY THIS PRAYER.

DEAR GOD, I'M IN NEED OF YOUR HELP, HELP ME RISE

ABOVE MY LITTLE EMOTIONS, HELP ME STAY THE COURSE,

HELP ME BE THE VESSEL THAT SHOWS YOUR LOVE AND

MERCY, HELP ME CONTINUE TO WALK IN YOUR FOOTPRINT

NOT THE ONES I ONCE MADE. GOD, SEE THROUGH THE

BEAUTIFUL SMILES OF THE WICKED AND MOST OF ALL

HELP ME LET THE WORLD KNOW GOD IS IN THE HOUSE, LET ME SAY IT AGAIN GOD IS IN THE HOUSE, AMEN, AMEN, AMEN.

Amen Wednesday worship, the workshop of God. within the workshop of God there is the (blind, death, and dumb) blind to his mighty power, death to his great words, and dumb to his sacrifice. we all have suffered these illnesses but today we enter the workshop of being released from those labels. I pray we all open our hearts minds and souls to the great works of our mighty God.
Trust in God first.

This year has come with a test, a lesson, and many blessings. I pray u all pass the test, understand your lesson, and receive your blessings for God says this shall pass. love you.
Gm welcome to super Sunday. I give all the thanks and praise to our great God for waking me to this super Sunday. Today you give it your all, in your

attempt to praise and serve God. So, make it known to someone that you appreciate and love them for God loves you. know that super Sunday gets u ready for magnificent Monday, then terrific
Tuesday, followed by wonderful Wednesday, tremendous
Thursday, fantastic Friday, just to get you to satisfying Saturday. love you all have a super day and be blessed.

With all that is going on in the world the word for the week is (positivity)

Welcome to magnificent Monday... Ok, we often ask God to talk to us... So, when he talks to you why you don't talk back. Gm this is God talking to you through me. He says, " my children come to me and I will show you the way. Come to me and I shall provide. Come to me and I will strengthen you. God says come to him always not just when you are broken and in need of a miracle. Come to me when the going is good for (I / GOD) got you there. come to me. Well, my family, I want you to go with me to God for he is the way. Talk to me. Tell us how good God has been to you. I want you all to know God has been wonderful to me, he brought me out of hell more than once and got me feeling so happy and loved today. thank you, God...

Gm all hey we are here inside of terrific Tuesday. What makes Tuesday so terrific. Well, if you asked, you have missed your first blessing of the day. For one we are here. He the all mighty has awakened us to begin an amazing day.

Dear God let us thank u for the first blessing of our day and for preparing us

for yet what is to come. I want to also thank you for your undying love. amen
So, to all my readers shout out loud thank u God for loving me that I may be able to show your love to others. Have a blessed day and know you are amazing as well.

Gm my beautiful people. Here's a wonderful Wednesday. I want u to tell me what makes Wednesday so wonderful to see.
For me, since I'm seeing it that tells me that God is still working on me. I have received my first blessing of the day. (won't he do it, Won't he do it) if you are (weak, worried, wondering,) just have faith that God will provide you with the things you need. but first, you must stop worrying, stop wondering, and stop feeling helpless and weak. then you add God into the front of all situations and

see the blessings start to unfold. Once again, I want to thank you God for all the chances you have given me to get it right, and for the never-ending blessings. AMEN, have a great day much love.

Here we go again welcome to tremendous Thursday. As we sit back and witness the tremendous works of our great God. We all have a testament to the great works of God in our own life. I'll share a little of mine. I know God has been with me my entire life because how else would I have survived some of my pains. He has taken me and walked with me through a fire, then through an empty cold part of my life, and molded me into this MAN I am today. I know he is real, some of life's events we could not have faced alone. He was there saying (my child stand up and let me give it to me and I will see u through) so my beautiful people give it to God and he will see u through. As we thank him for this day and every day hereafter remember to give it to God all the glory and praise. let us say AMEN, AMEN, AMEN

TGIF Fabulous, Forgiving, Faithful, Foundation Friday. As we build on our foundation, we remain faithful to our forgiving fabulous God. I know we get weak but remain rooted in your foundation. keep your faith in those moments you get lost, ask God to forgive u when you open that door to satin at times, be forever grateful to the mighty works of the lord.
Have a great day on this fabulous Friday. Peace

Let's say hello to Satisfying Saturday. In seven days, God created the world so one would think he was tired, well from my storybook God is forever working passing out blessings after blessings. The God I serve doesn't take time off, he does not call in sick, he doesn't say I got a doctor's appointment. So, I am going to serve him as he serves me, I'm going to praise him as he protects me, I am going to work for him as he worked on me. 24/7 every day all day. He has been my rock so I'll be his stone. so beautiful tell someone u love them today, wrap your arms around them and tell them to hold on hold on God got us. Amen, AMEN, AMEN, AMEN.

Hey, I'm moving slow but I'm here for super Sunday. Today what a great day. I have a question, why is Sunday set aside for praise for God. We were taught that we go to church on Sunday. (Why)? Well, let's change that, church and praise for God should be every day. Just as he provided for us every day. The church is where ever you are when you want to give him his praise. A new beginning, we are praising every day. Dear God as you continue to guide me on this journey of life. I want to thank you. thank you AMEN.

Come on down you are the next contestant on magnificent Monday. God has lots of gifts for you (life, love, family, favor, joy, peace) just to name a few. Having these things gives you meaning, then there is (sorrow, sadness, pain, loss) These things give you purpose. A purpose to do better, to aim high, to take him with you everywhere you go so that you continue with the good things in life. magnificent Monday gives me joy. love you all. Peace.

Gm terrific Tuesday, glad to see you. Today people, I want this to be (TRY ME TUESDAY). (Why)? Well, let's see. We have tried (alcohol) to get us through the pain and suffering, we have tried (drug after drug) to keep us happy, we have tried (woman after woman/man after man) to help us make it. Nothing is wrong with trying things but God is asking when you going to try (Him). God said I am he who supplies all your needs. You should come to me first and I shall work it out for you. He said I am the right drink that will help you see clearly, I am the best drug on the market for I will never let you down, I will always give you the right man/ woman just try me and see what I can do when u down and out try God don't pick up that phone and call no one get on your knees and call me. People let us try God he will do it. AMEN, AMEN, AMEN.

Welcome to a wonderful Wednesday. Let's see what happens with this wonderful day. As we move around this day let us focus on WORKING WITH

GOD WEDNESDAY. Yes, let's work for God just as you have worked to get them Jordans, that hair doo, that car. we work hard for all these materials that don't make you anything. but let's work for God for 30 days and see what you get. things money can't buy. happiness and peace. Peace out I'm going to work for God

Look up in the sky it's a terrific Thursday. Holidays, well my loved ones once again we are here in this season of giving. You have given everyone you love a gift from your heart but you left out one gift. You just couldn't find the right gift to give. Now, this person is thoughtful, caring, loving, powerful, understanding, forgiving, but you still couldn't think of the right gift. So, this person gets left out. Well, not this year. I want you all to join me in giving our great loving God the gift he gave us.

(life). I give my life to God for he has been the best gift-giver I know. so together let's say. dear God I give my life to you. AMEN, AMEN, AMEN.

Feeling fabulous Friday. These days can be brutal to some because of their trials and tribulations over the years. so today I want to send out a special prayer to those that are in need of encouragement know that God has wrapped his mighty arms around you and he got you and will continue to keep you. As you let that tear fall today know it's okay. no matter what u r going through it only can get better. I'm not saying merry Christmas instead I'm saying (I love you, I love you) so as God holds us, I want you all to hold that person or persons near you tight and say I love you. It is in gods, name we pray. AMEN, AMEN, AMEN.

Sanctified Saturday... growing up in my house Saturday was a day of cleaning lots of it, working in the garden. from sun up to sundown. lol. I look back and I want to give special thanks to those lessons. It helps build a certain kind of character within me. Just as they began to teach you about God. tell you about what connects u to all things in his wonderful creations. though we may stray at times those lessons remain within us. So, today take a moment to look within and reconnect with them lessons. find your connection with your God that he will step in and help you in your life. God is good all the time. Have a blessed day.
AMEN, AMEN, AMEN.

Gm Wow super superb Sunday is back again. Dear, God income to you today dirty and full of pain, I ask of you to clean us up dear God, and take away this pain. won't you rain down on us your water of love and healing. Open your flood gates and let your joy come pouring through. God, I knew when I closed my eyes to sleep last night there was a blessing waiting for me in the morning. you woke me up to your morning glory and I want to thank you, for all you do and have done for me (us). let us say AMEN, AMEN, AMEN.

Gm Monday. Today we are giving MEANING to our lives. To make our lives meaningful we have to begin to MAKE God a part of it, MANAGE it better, MOVE in a positive way, I want to thank God for my new direction in life, AMEN, AMEN, AMEN.

Gm terrific Tuesday. Let's put on our THINKING TUESDAY so we can make it terrific. First, I have a question. (what makes you family?). It's not blood that's for sure. Blood only makes you related. family is (in my words) an act of care, love, and devotion. What I want for me I want for u. Now let's move it to the spiritual realm. what family are you a part of (GODS family or that WICKED family) God has shown you that he wants you in his family every day he wakes you up so show him you are a part of his family by the things you do for others with a simple (thank you, hello, etc.) God's family gets blessings. Amen.

Wonderful Wednesday. Gm, this morning I'm filled with questions, first question, (Am I worthy of all these blessings) the second question (what have I done to warrant these wonderful blessings). Just a couple to make or get you to think. we always are on the receiving end of God's love and blessings. So, today let's give God the praise for what he continues to do for us. Oh, wonderful God, I want to thank you for never letting me down even in the times I wasn't worthy of your blessings, I want to thank you God for always holding on to me. never letting go. AMEN, AMEN, AMEN.

Gm Thursday. Stop looking back and drive off into a better you. Moving ahead you take a moment reflect on your lessons and blessing and move forward never taking with you that which you don't need (stress, mess, sickness, etc.) It is not called throw bk Thursday for nothing. So, we throw all the stress and mess and sickness back to who and what it belongs to. (satin). Thank you, God, for moving us ahead

keeping us blessed favored, and healthy. love you all...
Peace... AMEN, AMEN, AMEN

WORDS

There once was a word never spoken, then a cry that went unheard, while screaming loudly and saying nothing we fight for words. Words where do they come from. Out of an empty soul they are full of disbelief, from a brilliant mind they are conceived from lies, but the words we follow to a dreadful abyss or to a magical fairy tale. Words .... Words. Word.

"BE ENCOURAGED"

I want to thank everyone for their support and encouragement in keeping me focused and moving forward.